PARENTING

G. RON NORTON

A SPECTRUM BOOK

PRENTICE-HALL, INC., Englewood Cliffs, New Jersey 07632

Library of Congress Cataloging in Publication Data
Norton, Ron.
Parenting

(A Spectrum Book)
Includes index.
1. Children—Management.   2. Problem children.
3. Behavior modification.   I. Title.
HQ769.N645 1977   649′.1   76-30846
ISBN 0-13-650069-2 pbk.

A Spectrum Book

Printed in the United States of America

10   9   8   7   6   5   4   3   2   1

Prentice-Hall International, Inc., *London*
Prentice-Hall of Australia Pty. Limited, *Sydney*
Prentice-Hall of Canada, Ltd., *Toronto*
Prentice-Hall of India Private Limited, *New Delhi*
Prentice-Hall of Japan, Inc., *Tokyo*
Prentice-Hall of Southeast Asia Pte. Ltd., *Singapore*
Whitehall Books Limited, *Wellington, New Zealand*

Contents

iii

80 29

2

Talking With Your Children: Improving Communication 15

3

Talking With Your Children: Helping to Solve Problems 29

4

Punishment: The First Line of Defense   42

5

Making Punishment Effective   55

6

Using Rewards to Create a Positive Relationship 70

What Are Rewards?
How Do Rewards Work?

7

Using Rewards Effectively 89

Teaching New Behavior
Maintaining Behavior That Has Been Learned
Intentionally Not Rewarding
Control and Rebellion
Conclusions

8

Providing Cues for Positive Behavior 106

How Stimuli Influence Behavior
Managing Stimuli to Produce Appropriate Behavior
Using Stimulus Influence Concepts
  to Improve Parent-Child Relationships

9

Children Learn by Observing Others 130

How Children Learn to Imitate
What Can a Child Learn by Observing Others?

10

Using Observational Learning Methods
To Change Behavior   145

11

Using the Child's Imagination   159

12

Professional Help for Disturbed Children   176

Preface

When I began to write this book, I had planned to write a "how to" manual that might help parents more successfully interact with their children. But as I worked through the drafts of several chapters I realized that most parents are doing quite a good job with their children and that the material I had written might be unnecessary for most parents. I then thought that many parents might be interested in knowing not only some different ways of interacting with their children but how children learn. This, I thought, might improve their relationship with their children, and they could also see why what they are doing has the effects it has on their children. I've found that this idea meets with the approval of most parents. I know I dislike being told to do something to my child without knowing why I am to do it. I have this feeling when I take my child to a doctor when he has a cold. The doctor says, "Give him two of these pills every four hours and keep him warm." "Why? What will happin if I do? What will happen if I don't? Are there other ways of handling the situation that are better?"

Most of us don't ask these questions of our doctor. We assume that he knows best, and he probably does, but we want to know why he feels this is the best, and he probably does, but we want to know why he feels this is the best treatment for our child. After all, it is our child and we are concerned with doing the right thing. Maybe if we knew more about what was wrong and how to change the problem we could do a better job. I've tried to use this logic throughout the book. I want to show you ways of interacting with your child that I and other people have found helpful, but I also want you to know why I think the ideas will be of value.

Although this book was specifically written for parents, I hope it will be of use to many "substitute" or surrogate parents such as nurses, teachers, grandparents, and others who work with children. The role of these surrogate parents is often more than just providing assistance to the teaching of the parents: It is a very important, individual contribution to the growth and development of children. In fact, for some children it is these surrogate parents who provide a stable, caring, learning environment. Because surrogate parents are so important in teaching children how to interact with the world, I hope they will also benefit from this book. I have used the terms *parent* and *parenting* to describe not only the role and activities of parents but also the role and activities of surrogate parents.

I've tried to present the material in the chapters in a logical and sequential manner so that what you learn in the early chapters will be of value for helping you to understand more completely the material in later chapters. Throughout the book I have used a large number of examples to illustrate the concepts I've described. It is hoped these will give you an idea of how the concepts might be applied with your own children. In addition, I've enclosed some of the more important examples and other information in boxes. The boxes are used to illustrate how various childrearing ideas have been used by professionals. Most of these examples are illustrations of how some severe behavior problems have been treated. Other boxes present material that might be of immediate importance to parents.

To help you to put into practice the concepts you have been reading about, I've included an exercise at the end of each chapter. The exercises will allow you either to evaluate your interactions with your children or to actually practice trying new ways of interacting with your children. I hope you will find these exercises informative, worthwhile, and enjoyable.

Finally, because I feel both parents should take active parenting roles, I've used examples and descriptions throughout the book where I sometimes refer to the male parent and sometimes the female parent. I've used this form as a way of trying to involve both parents in the material.

ACKNOWLEDGMENTS

I have had excellent assistance in writing this book, and I would like to acknowledge publicly some of the people who have helped me. First, two people read and reread the various chapters and made important comments that have helped me greatly. They are my wife, Judy, who not only helped me write about the methods I've described but who has very successfully used them with our two sons; and Professor G. E. Allen, who has been a friend and reviewer of my work for so long that I often wonder whose ideas I'm describing, his or mine. In addition, I would like to acknowledge the help given me by Drs. Howard Sloane and George Endo. Both have read and commented on several chapters. Those chapters would have been far less exact and interesting without their help. I would also thank Dr. Claude Grant, chairman of the Deparment of Educational Psychology, University of utah, for providing me with the space and secretarial assistance necessary for writing this book. A special thank-you is necessary for Mrs. Virginia Hart, who translated my scribbles into a beautifully typed manuscript.

Finally, I would like to dedicate this book to my two sons, Marshall and Peter, who seem to understand almost instinctively the ideas I've described in this book and who seem to use them better and more positively than most people I've met.

G. RON NORTON
teaches in the Psychology Department
at the University of Winnipeg in Canada

1

Parents And Children

Wouldn't it be nice if we could be perfect parents? Our children would grow up happy and able to get along well with other people. We parents would be happy that we didn't have the problems other parents have with their children. Yes, it would be nice, but most of us have occasional problems with our children. Most of us try hard to do the right things with our children, but things don't always go the way we want. When this happens we often feel guilty. It seems everyone has advice to offer us. Our parents and our friends all seem to know just what we should do.

I don't know what a perfect parent is; I'm not even sure that such a person exists. What might work for one parent might not work for another. Besides, times change, and what might have been good parenting practices for our parents and grandparents might not work now. Nor might the things we did with our children as infants be effective with them as preschoolers or teenagers. Parenting is a complex task that requires sensitivity and a willingness to look at what we are doing to our children—and to change if necessary.

One thing that is certain is that, within rather broad limits, some styles of parenting are generally more effective than others in producing children that are happy and socially self-reliant. Notice that I stress that these styles are *generally* better. Some parents, for reasons that are unclear as yet, can act in ways that we might expect would produce unhappy children and yet are parents of children who are happy, socially competent, and well adjusted. Again, what works for one parent might not work for others.

However, after stressing this point, I would like to present to you the results of some important research that has been done on styles of parenting. We will see that some of these styles are generally more effective than others. After that, I would like to present what can be called the "Children's Bill of Rights." I think that you will be interested to see that normal children see their parents as doing the things that research has shown good parents already do. After we've considered the styles of parenting and the Children's Bill of Rights, I would like to describe several ideas or themes that will be developed more fully in later chapters. These themes are based on the findings of what are good styles of parenting, the Children's Bill of Rights, and my own work with parents (and my own experience as a parent). I believe that these concepts can help you to evaluate your role as a parent and the effect your behavior has on your children. Hopefully, you will find some or all the ideas helpful in becoming a better parent.

STYLES OF PARENTING

An important study of parenting styles by Dr. Diana Baumrind has shown that they can be grouped into three main categories. Baumrind studied a large number of preschool children and determined their behavioral adjustment by observing them in play situations, by talking to their teachers, and by using psychological tests. She then interviewed their parents to find out how parents of children at various levels of adjustment interacted with their children. From the interviews and observations in the parent's homes, Baumrind described three patterns of parenting. Read Baumrind's description below of each of the three categories and decide which category best describes your style of parenting. Then, without reading further, decide which type of parent you would like to be. You might be in for some surprise when you read what effects each style of parenting has on the behavioral growth of children. For convenience, Baumrind referred to the parent as "she" and the child as "he," but the results were equally true for both male and female parents and children.

Authoritarian Parent

The authoritarian parent attempts to shape, control, and evluate the behavior and attitudes of her child in accordance with a set standard of conduct, usually an absolute standard, theologically motivated and formulated by a higher authority. She values obedience as a virtue and favors punitive, forceful measures to curb self-will at points where the child's actions or beliefs conflict with what she thinks is right conduct. She believes in inculcating such instrumental values as respect for authority, respect for work and for the preservation of order and traditional structure. She does not encourage verbal give and take, believing that the child should accept her word for what is right.

Authoritative Parent

Authoritative parents attempt to direct the child's activities but in a rational, issue-oriented manner. She encourages verbal give and take, and shares with the child the reasoning behind her policy. She values both expressive and instrumental attributes, both autonomous self-will and disciplined conformity. Therefore, she exerts firm control at points of parent-child divergences, but does not hem the child in with restrictions. She recognizes her own special rights as an adult, but also the child's individual interests and special ways. The authoritative parent affirms the child's present qualities, but also sets standards for future conduct. She uses reason as well as power to achieve her objectives. She does not base her decisions on group consensus or the individual child's desires, but also does not regard herself as infallible or divinely inspired.

Permissive Parent

Permissive parents attempt to behave in a nonpunitive, acceptant, and affirmitive manner toward the child's impulses, desires, and actions. She consults with him about policy decisions and gives explanations for family rules. She makes few demands for household responsibility and orderly behavior. She presents herself to the child as a resource for him to use as he wishes, not as an active agent responsible for shaping or altering his ongoing or future behavior. She allows the child to regulate his own abilities as much as possible, avoids the exercise of control, and does not encourage him to obey externally-defined standards. She attempts to use reason, but not overpower to accomplish her ends.[1]

Which parent type did you decide you were most like? Which would you want to be? You probably found that you fit some, but not all, of the statements in each of the categories. In fact, these are just general tendencies. Parenting styles are far more complex than was described in the three categories. Different parents who might generally be considered authoritative, for example, may differ on several other dimensions. One parent may be more likely to be considered a nonconformist than another. Yet, both are authoritative in their interactions with their children. Baumrind has, in fact, greatly elaborated the three basic styles of parenting by including several other important dimensions. Similarly, other people who have studied parent/child relationships have described other patterns of parenting and their effects on children. However, the three categories—authoritarian, permissive, and authoritative—provide a simple and convenient framework for discussing how different styles of parenting can affect the development of children.

What are the effects of each style of parenting on the behavior of children? Baumrind found that the parents of children who were the most self-reliant, self-controlled, explorative, and content were the parents whom she described as authori*tative*. The children of authori*tarian* parents were discontented, withdrawn, and distrustful. One of the most interesting findings, however, is that the children who were least explorative, self-reliant, and self-controlled were children of permissive parents.

These findings led Baumrind to propose that "firm enforcement of policies in which the behavior desired by the parent is positively reinforced and behavior regarded as deviant by the parent is negatively

---

[1]Baumrind, D. Current Patterns of Parental Authority. *Developmental Psychology Monographs,* 1971, Vol. 4, No. 1, Part 2.

reinforced, facilitates the development in the child of socially responsible behavior.''

The findings of Baumrind's study are generally consistent with findings by other psychologists. Some additional information and elaboration of parent styles and their effects on children come from a large research project with mothers of school-age children, by psychiatrist Robert Sears and his co-workers. They found that while some parents generally used punishment or harsh methods to discipline their children, other mothers who were more positive, although they occasionally used punishment, were much more likely to encourage good behavior by rewarding the child for being good. The frequent use of harsh procedures seemed to produce more problem behaviors in children. In addition, punishment was not all that effective for doing what was intended—improving the behavior of the child. Did the mothers who used harsh methods and those who were more positive show other differences in personality? Yes! Sears found that mothers who chose to make frequent use of praise and other rewards were above average in (1) warmth and affection shown to their children, (2) satisfaction with being wives and mothers, (3) esteem they felt for their husbands, and (4) permissiveness regarding their children's sexual behavior.[2]

When we combine the findings of Baumrind's study with those of Sears', an interesting picture emerges. Parents of children who are self-reliant, content, and relatively free from problem behaviors are parents who don't use punishment excessively to control their children's behavior. True, they discipline and punish their children, but their discipline is more positive (rewarding good behavior rather than punishing bad behavior); they direct their child's behavior, but use reason rather than appeal to authority for deciding what and when to punish; and finally, these parents are warmer and more involved with their children and with each other than are more punitive parents.

So far we've looked at different styles of parenting and seen that they have different effects on the behavior of children. What about the child? How do normal children perceive their parents? Do they differ in their perceptions from children who have problems?

[2]Sears, R. R., Macoby, E., and Levin, H. *Patterns of Child Rearing.* New York: Harper & Row, 1957.

CHILDREN'S BILL OF RIGHTS

F.S. Schaefer gave normal and delinquent boys a questionnaire designed to measure their perceptions of their parents.[3] His results were very interesting—normal and delinquent children saw their parents as acting in very different ways. Normal children saw their parents as being more directive than did the delinquent boys. The delinquent boys rated their parents as being more permissive. When parents of delinquents were seen as trying to control their children's behavior, they were seen to control by making their children feel guilty.

The differences in the children's perceptions of their parents' behavior was more complex than just being controlling or permissive. The two groups of boys saw their parents as also differing in the amount of affection they gave and their willingness to discuss matters with their children. The parents of normal children were seen as being more affectionate and more willing to discuss matters in a give-and-take manner. A possible factor underlying the differences in how normal and delinquent children perceived their parents might be if the parents were consistent and harmonious in their interactions with their children. When Schaefer compared the boys' perceptions of their mothers and fathers, he found that normal boys rated their parents as being far more consistent and harmonious than did the delinquents.

When we consider the differing perceptions of parenting behaviors, we see that normal children perceive their parents in ways that are consistent with how Baumrind and others say good parents should interact with children. In fact, these similarities could be expressed as a set of parenting guidelines or a "Children's Bill of Rights." Parents should:

1. Be consistent in their interactions with their children.
2. Treat their children with affection.
3. Concentrate on their children's good points, not their failings.
4. Treat their children as individuals who have their own point of view.

[3]Schaefer, F.S. Children's Reports of Parental Behavior: An Inventory. *Child Development,* 1965, Vol. 36, pp. 413–421.

5. Be understanding and tolerant of their children's behavior yet provide direction when necessary.

Two interesting themes develop when we compare the style of parenting that seems to be correlated with children that are happiest and most socially reliant and the items listed in the Children's Bill of Rights. The first theme is the stress on positive interaction between parents and the children. The authoritative parent tries to recognize her child as an individual with a "mind of his own" and encourages him to express his individuality within the limits of socially acceptable patterns of behavior. These patterns of behavior are not necessarily those imposed by some religious structure or defined as correct by some such external authority. The authoritative parent uses reason and logic and relies less on advice from external authorities in deciding if her child's behavior is appropriate or inappropriate. In addition, the authoritative parent tries to explain to the child the logic behind her actions. If the actions seem unreasonable to the child, the child is encouraged to express his feelings or reasons for his behavior. By doing this the authoritative parent affirms the child as a capable individual, is able to direct the child's present behavior, and can set conditions so that the child is likely to be socially responsible in his future behaviors. The relationship, then, between parent and child is one of positive give and take and, to a certain extent, that of a teacher and pupil, where the parent tries to guide the child's behavior.

The Children's Bill of Rights confirms this approach—at least from the child's point of view—by specifying that children want to be recognized as individuals. They should not be subjected to the whims and irrationalities of parents, but should be treated fairly and positively. More than that, there is a plea for a positive, understanding relationship between parent and child. The Children's Bill of Rights affirms the parents' role of guiding the child as he learns about his world, but asks that this guidance be within a framework of fairness, tolerance, and honesty.

The second theme, which is integrally connected with the first, is the emphasis of parent as teacher. A child, although born with a complexity that we are just now beginning to appreciate, behaves largely in accordance with how he is taught. It might be nice to think that a child comes preprogrammed from birth to behave in certain ways—it would put less stress on parents to teach the child. But this is obviously not so. Numerous studies have shown that within the child's biological limits, his behavior is likely to be similar to those who are responsible for raising him. If his parents are people who enjoy sports and if the child is physically able to enjoy sports, he too will probably enjoy sports. If, on the other hand, his parents dislike physical activities and emphasize more sedentary activities, the child is more likely to develop similar interests. This shows us that, intentionally or not, parents are constantly teaching their children how to interact with the world. The authoritative parent accepts this responsibility and tries to do the best job possible. The parent will try to encourage the child to behave in ways that are instrumental in achieving success and happiness in the child's world. This direction is often firm, but well thought out. This is consistent with what the Children's Bill of Rights asks parents to do—to encourage the child's good features and to give him helpful information.

These themes can be considered together as a set of guidelines specifying the rights and responsibilities of parents as well as of children. A parent has the responsibility of trying to establish a warm, positive relationship with his child. In addition, the parent has the responsibility to guide the child's behavior in ways that will allow him to become a happy, competent child—and later, a happy, competent adult. The parent also has the right to direct the child's behavior, which means the right to discipline when necessary. This right includes the expectation that the child will not abuse the freedoms that the parent allows.

The child has the right to a warm, positive home environment that will encourage him to become socially competent. The child also has the right to be considered an individual capable of making decisions about his life. These decisions should be fairly considered by the parent.

The child also has the responsibility to behave within well-founded guidelines and to respect the effort that his parents put into directing his behavior.

RESPONSIBILITY AND STYLE OF CHILD REARING

This book is written for parents and is concerned with ways of interacting with children so as to encourage them to become happy and socially competent. It is necessary to keep in mind that the ways parents interact with their children should be carefully scrutinized. It might be easy to read this book or other similar books in child rearing and get the message that to have a happy child all that must be done is to follow the guidelines laid out in the book. This attitude implies that the child is the one who must change his behavior, which is not always the case. Sometimes the behavior of the child is quite appropriate, but the parent, for whatever reason, reacts inappropriately. For example, a parent in one of my counseling groups was concerned with his wife's reaction to their children. The children, according to the father, were reasonably well behaved, but the mother was unrealistic in her demands on the children. The children could not play in the house because they might mess up the house; they couldn't laugh or talk loudly because it upset the mother. In this case it became clear that the problem in the home was not with the children's inappropriate behavior, but with the behavior of the mother. If I had helped the father to establish a program of interacting with the children that was consistent with what the mother wanted, I feel I would have been wrong. What was necessary, and what was finally done, was to develop a program that would change the mother's reactions to the children. This was successfully accomplished, and the relationship between the parents and the children (and between husband and wife) greatly improved without any substantial change in the children's behavior. I mention this example to show that a parent who is unhappy with his child's behavior can use the ideas described in this book in a way that might, in fact, produce a child that is not only more unhappy, but whose behavior with others would be inappropriate. When we wish to change our child's behavior, it is important to ask, "Why?" For whom is the behavior a problem? Is the behavior a problem for the child in that if he continues to behave as he is, he will lose friends? Or is the child's behavior a problem only for the parent? In the above example the way the children were behaving was appropriate, but the problem was the mother's unrealistic ideas of how children should behave. Another example of misidentification of who has the problem is the parent who expects his child to behave in ways that the child is either incapable of or is not physically mature enough to do. A father I knew had aspired to be a major league baseball player. He never made the grade because he was not good enough (although he wouldn't admit it), but insisted that his child become a major leaguer. The child was a frail, poorly coordinated child who was equally incapable of excelling at baseball. But the father would daily take the child out and pitch to him, bat him grounders, and yell at the child when he didn't perform up to the father's expectations. The father, of course, blamed the child for not trying and was heard to remark time and time again,

"What do you do with a kid like that? I give him more time than any other father and he doesn't appreciate it. He just won't try." Where does the problem lie? With the child? Not in this case. The child didn't try, that's true, but it was because whatever he did wasn't good enough for his father. The child hated playing baseball with his father. All his father did was yell at him. Can you see the relationship that was developing between the father and the child? Not a very warm, positive one, was it? The father was discouraged and unhappy with his child, and the boy was afraid and unhappy with his father.

A parent who is concerned with doing the best possible job of being a good parent should recognize that sometimes parent-child problems are due to the parent's inappropriate expectations and feelings about how the child should behave. It is very difficult to specify rules for determining where the problem lies. Some parents might honestly view a child's behavior as inappropriate while other parents would see the same behavior as being quite acceptable. Who is right is partly a moral problem and may be beyond the scope of this book. At other times, the question can be answered by resorting to convention. Do most people feel the child's behavior is appropriate? If so, then there might be reason for the parent to reconsider his expectations. This certainly does not mean that other people are always right and the parent wrong. It is just a way of checking your perceptions of right and wrong against some consensual standard.

If you have asked the question "Do others feel that my child's behavior is appropriate?" and found that others disagree with your feelings, then the next step is to try to find out why you disagree. You may still feel, after logically and honestly looking at the problem, that your position is correct. If so, then by all means do what you feel is right. You probably wouldn't feel comfortable if you had allowed your judgment to be swayed by no other reason than convention. Besides, if you did decide to go along with the others for reasons of just conforming, you probably wouldn't do a good job of handling your child's problem. You would still have nagging doubts which could interfere with your being an effective parent.

Another way of approaching the problem of who should change— the parent or the child—is to ask: "For whom is the child's behavior a problem?" If you can honestly answer that the behavior is a problem only because it is an inconvenience for you, then the problem might be yours and not the child's. If, on the other hand, you can honestly say that the child's behavior is interfering with his social relationships with others and that the behavior is of no real value to him, then the behavior should be considered a problem for the child and it is he who should change.

The question of who is right and who is wrong is a question that is usually asked by an authori*tative* parent. He is concerned with the reasons for his behavior and the behavior of his child. An authori*tarian* parent would not have this problem: he is always right and has some authority (be it religion or some other agency) to back him up. Likewise, the permissive parent would not be troubled by this question. His child would be allowed to engage in the behavior regardless of the reasons.

Most parents are concerned enough to ask themselves the question of who is right and who is wrong some of the time. The question might come in many forms, such as "Am I being too hard on Johnny?" or "Maybe I'm being foolish not to let Susan do this or that."

LABELS:
WHAT IS GOOD AND WHAT IS BAD?

Can any behavior be categorically labeled good or bad? We might think of murder as unconditionally bad and giving to charity as always good, but there are times and places when the value of these behaviors might be different. There are different people for whom the labels of good and bad might apply to quite different types of behaviors. I'm sure if you think about it you can find people with whom you've disagreed over the value you've placed on a behavior. A good example of this is capital punishment. Some people feel that it is immoral for the state to take a person's life. Others feel that capital punishment can be justified because it removes undesirables from our society. Whichever way you feel about the issue, I'm sure you know others who disagree with you. The same is true with child rearing. Some people feel that children should be taught the common amenities, such as saying "Please" and "Thank you"; other parents might feel these are not very important. In other words, placing a label of right or wrong requires making a value judgment—a decision by someone that the behavior should be encouraged or discouraged. Because people place different values on particular behaviors, I've tried to use terms that have less emotion or value emphasis attached to them when describing behaviors or ways to change behavior. Although the terms I've chosen still require a value judgment, they have the advantage of being tied less to conventions and more to situations. Therefore, I've chosen to use the words *appropriate* and *inappropriate* when describing situations or behavior change techniques. I've chosen to use these words because they seem to be less emotionally laden and because they can be more easily used to refer to a *behavior* in a *specific situation*.

CONCLUSIONS

There is very close agreement between parenting patterns that many psychologists have found important for producing children who are happy and socially capable and what we have termed the "Children's Bill of Rights." Both stress positive interactions between parents and children based on mutual trust, reason, and affection. It is also important to note that neither the psychologists who have studied parenting patterns nor the children who were interviewed felt that punishment was necessarily bad. Punishment is undesirable as a parenting tool only when it is missed. In fact, the misuse of punishment as well as an authoritarian attitude toward teaching children defined the authoritarian parenting pattern, one most likely to produce children who are unhappy and socially unreliant.

Children need direction to learn about their world and to discover which behaviors are socially acceptable and which not. Most of this direction can be accomplished by using positive methods described in later chapters, but sometimes more aversive methods are required. Overly permissive parents are unlikely to give either positive or negative directions, with the result that their children will not have the necessary skills to interact with others. This can only lead to unhappiness. If the proper parenting methods are used, there is a good likelihood that a child will grow up happy, socially reliant, and able to establish meaningful relationships with others. These methods most likely to produce these behaviors are those based on a rational understanding, warmth, love, and proper direction.

EXAMPLE 1.1

The Child-Abusing Parent

Why does a parent physically abuse his child? Fortunately most parents don't beat their children so severely that the child requires medical attention. But some do. Why?

In a review of the research that has been done on child-abusing parents Drs. J. J. Spinetta and D. Rigler described some characteristics of parents who physically abuse their children. People often think of child-abusing parents as insane or at least severely disturbed, but this doesn't seem to be the case for most parents who abuse their children. Spinneta and Rigler cited several factors which might influence a person to abuse his child. One important factor is the way in which the parent was raised when he was a child. Most people who abuse their children were also abused as children. They were raised in an emotionally cold and rejecting family environment. As children they were often abused and neglected, physically or emotionally. In other words, they were raised in the same way they are treating their children.

Abusing parents, possibly because of their upbringing, tend to have certain misconceptions about the nature of child rearing and tend to fall into a common pattern:

1. They demand a great deal from their infants and children, often before the child is capable of engaging in the demanded behavior.
2. Child-abusing mothers may have severely frustrated dependency needs and an inability to empathize with their children.
3. Child-abusing parents tend to disregard the needs of their children.
4. Child-abusing parents not only consider punishment a proper disciplinary measure, but strongly defend their right to use physical force.

Not everyone fitting these descriptions will abuse his children but the evidence indicates that people who lack warmth, have mistaken notions of child rearing, and who themselves were abused as children might, under some conditions, severely abuse their child. Hopefully, these parents can learn better ways of interacting with their children.

From J.J. Spinetta and D. Rigler, The Child-Abusing Parent. *Psychological Bulletin,* 1972, vol. 77, pp. 296-304.

EXERCISE

If you have decided that you would like to become more authoritative in your interactions with your children, you might wish to consider the following ideas:

1. When an authoritative parent tells her child that he can't do something, how is it said? For most of us it is too easy just to say, "Don't do that." If the child asks why, we might say something like "Because I told you you can't." How does this help the child learn about why he should or should not engage in different actions? It doesn't. All it does is tell him he can't engage in the behavior. An authoritative parent would be more likely to say, "Don't do that. If you touch the stove it will burn your finger. You don't want to hurt yourself, do you?" Here, the parent has not only told the child he shouldn't engage in the behavior, but also the reasons for not engaging in the behavior. Usually, the best reasons are those that specify the possible consequences of the behavior. In this case the consequences would have been a burn and pain.

2. What about when your child makes a request of you that you feel is unreasonable, but the child feels it is appropriate? How would an authoritative parent handle this? For example, suppose your child said, "How come I have to go to bed at 8:30? Johnny doesn't have to. I want to stay up, too!" An authoritative parent would recognize the child's feelings, but try to explain to the child why she feels the child's request is inappropriate. The parent might say, for example, "Honey, when you stay up late you are very tired in the mornings. Tomorrow is a school day and you should be rested for school. I'll tell you what. If you want, you can stay up a little later on Friday and Saturday nights. Do you think that would be okay?" Again, the parent has tried to explain to the child why she feels he should engage in a particular behavior.

So far we've seen that an authoritative parent not only directs her children's behavior, but also tries to let the child know why the parent acts as she does. Consider your own interactions with your children. For the next few days try to keep track of how often you use direction with or without explaining why you feel what you have said or done is appropriate. If you find that you are not explaining your directions to your children, you may wish to change. Directions with explanations provide the child with additional information that he might be able to use later. Directions alone just tell the child what he is to do or not do without a guiding rationale. This tends to be specific to the situation and does not provide the child with information he can use later.

2

Talking With Your Children: Improving Communication

I find that I'm often surprised at some of the things my children say about their lives away from home. They have friends I've never met and interests that I've never encouraged. Each of them, like other children, can seem to be two different people—the child we know at home and the person he is away from home. Sometimes we never really get to know these other persons. We should; they can be complex, very interesting children who are fun to know.

Besides, there are other advantages to knowing what our children do away from home. Sometimes the things they do and say at home carry over from their life away from home. Knowing the things that happen away from home can help us understand more completely our child's behavior at home. If, for example, our children do or say something that we've never seen or heard before, we might find that the roots of their actions lie in their interactions with friends or teachers. The better we know our children, the better able we are to help direct this behavior and to help them learn to live in this complex world.

Your child will also appreciate your interest. If you can more completely understand his behavior, then the chances are that you will be more fair and understanding in your interactions with him. Things that he does that may anger you might be more logical and appropriate if you understand the way his other world has affected his behavior at home. A good example of this is the child who comes home from school and is rude to his younger brother. At first, you might be inclined to get mad and punish your child, but if you were aware that he had been having trouble being accepted by a group of children at school, you might react differently. His rudeness would still be inappropriate, but the way in which you handle the situation might be different. Rather than punishing the child by sending him to his room and possibly increasing his feelings of rejection, you might wish to sit down and talk to him about his actions toward his little brother. Most children appreciate a parent who is tolerant of occasional misdeeds resulting from what he considers to be unfair treatment. Remember, tolerance was one of the things listed in the "Children's Bill of Rights" in the first chapter. We're often not at our best when things are bugging us—and *neither are children*! Try to understand their point of view. It could help your relationship with your child.

How can you get to know your child better? Most of us try and most of us succeed, at least some of the time. But how can we insure a better understanding and a more open and positive relationship? The answer on one hand is very simple, but on the other hand is much more complex: Try talking to your child. Sound simple? Yes, of course it does, but for those of us who have tried unsuccessfully, it is not such a simple solution. The answer is, then, not only just talking to your child, but talking to him in a way that will increase understanding and friendship and allow you to give him better direction in his activities.

This chapter will explain ways of talking with your child that will increase mutual understanding and tolerance.

HOW DO YOU TALK TO YOUR CHILD?

Since most of our interactions with other people, including our children, are at the verbal or talk level, it is important to know how to talk to others so that we communicate effectively. We can all think of cases where we have said something to a person and they have inferred a meaning that we did not intend. The same is true when we talk with our children. We can, with every intent to be understanding, say something that the child interprets in a different way. The result is hard feelings. What causes these problems in communication between parent and child?

Although there are probably a large number of reasons for poor communication, let's look at three that are very important. The first problem is that words can have different meanings for different people. For example, suppose your child came into a room where you were writing an important letter and said, "Dad, can you . . ."—and you interrupt him and say, "Please, Johnny, don't bother me." How might this be differently interpreted by you and your child? You might have meant, "Wait for just one minute until I finish this sentence, then I'll talk to you." The child may have felt punished and understood you to mean, "Don't bug me, kid. I haven't time to bother myself with you." A simple case of misunderstanding, but it is likely to have consequences that will affect future interactions between you and your child.

Another reason for different interpretations of words is when a parent tells a child not to do something. The parent might think he is teaching the child how to behave properly, but the child may see this as having a different meaning: He may see the parent as being mean and unfair. For example, late on Sunday evening your child says, "Mom, may I go over to Jim's and play?" Because of the late hour and because your child has school the next morning you say, "No, of course you can't!" The child may feel he is being punished (but doesn't know why) and that visiting his friend is bad. What you meant when you said "no" was that it was late and the child had school tomorrow. Because you did not explain why you refused to let your child go, the child was left with one set of feelings and you another.

A second problem of communication lies not in the words, but when and where the words are said. A child who is upset or who, in the past, has frequently been verbally punished or put down will interpret your message quite differently than if the child is not upset or has had more positive talk interactions with his parent. Imagine a situation where the parent, for whatever reason, is constantly on the child's back and the main type of talk the parent uses is negative. When the child talks to his parents he expects to be told "no" and he will interpret the parent's refusal not as a legitimate refusal, but another case of unfairness. A parent to be effective in communicating "no" to a child must also be a parent who is effective in positively communicating with his child. A child whose parents encourage appropriate behavior and explain their refusals are more likely to effectively communicate with their children than are more negative parents.

A third problem is the emotion shown when a parent says something to a child. A parent who says "no" in a calm, friendly manner will communicate something quite different from the parent who shows anger when saying "no." In the first case the child might accept the parent's statement and let it go at that. In the second case the child might get mad or upset with the parent's refusal. The difference in the child's reaction is important to the parent-child relationship. One child has negative feelings toward his parent, the other doesn't.

When we try to analyze the effects our talk behavior has on the child, it is convenient to think of our talking as stimuli or cues that have different effects on the behavior of our children. Some verbal cues are more likely to control or produce good behavior than others. Words such as "no," "don't," and "stop that" are more likely to cause negative feelings than more positive phrases such as "that's nice" and "I like that." The negative words have an even greater effect if they are combined with the other two stimulus conditions (the situation and the emotion of the parent) mentioned above. Basically, positive talk stimuli produce positive reactions and negative talk stimuli cause negative reactions. The more positive you are, the more positive will be the child's response; the more negative you are, the more negative the child's response.

What cues do you provide when talking to your child? Most of us vary in the amount of negative or positive cues we use when talking to our children. Sometimes, and on some topics, we are very positive, and at other times and on other topics we are more negative. It may be kind of interesting to do a self-analysis to see if we tend to be generally positive or negative in out talk interactions with our children. One way of finding out is to monitor or record your talk behavior. It might give you some insights into your relationship with your children. I strongly suspect that if you use positive talk cues with your child, you also have a warm, positive relationship. Test yourself. Chart your negative and positive comments to your children. You might be surprised at what you find. You might also decide this is an area you want to improve.

Self-Charting Positive and Negative Comments

The best way of finding out how often you use positive and negative comments with your children is to actually count your comments. To do this, select a time of day, such as dinnertime, when you are likely to verbally interact with your children. Then devise some way of recording your interactions. A good way to record your verbal interaction would be to put a tape recorder in an inconspicuous place and turn it on during the recording period. The tape recorder, if placed in the area of maximum interaction, will record the things you say and the things your children say. This will give an objective record of your interactions during that particular time. You can use this record as an indicator of your interactions.

A word of caution: People, when self-recording, tend to be on their good behavior. You'll probably say more positive things and fewer negative things while you are recording than you normally would. Take this into consideration when evaluating your interaction.

When you have finished recording your verbal interactions with your children, sit down and listen to the tape. While you are listening to the tape have a pencil and paper at hand. Mark the paper into three columns; the first columm will be "Positive Comments," the second column "Negative Comments," and the third column "Neutral or No Comments." Then turn on the tape recorder. Every ten seconds stop the tape and decide if your talking behavior during the ten-second interval was mostly positive, mostly negative, or neutral, and make a check mark in the appropriate column. Do this regardless of the circumstances or your child's behavior. What we're interested in is your talking behavior, not your child's behavior. Evaluating your talk behavior can be difficult and often aversive. We don't like to admit to bad things about ourselves. Another thing you should try not to do is to make value judgments about your talking behavior. You might find yourself saying or thinking, "That was a negative comment, but I was right in being negative." After you've recorded your behavior for the totality of the tape, think about the circumstances surrounding your comments, but don't do it while you are recording. What you should be trying to do is get a general index of your talking behavior.

If properly done, these records should give you a general idea of your current patterns of interacting with your child. It is likely that you might select either a good or bad day for recording. Maybe, to get a more accurate record, you should record your interactions for several days. You might consider recording your behavior over a period of a least five days. This would be more likely to give you an accurate picture of the ways you verbally interact with your children.

If you don't have access to a tape recorder, you can accomplish the same thing with paper and a pencil. Every time you notice yourself making a positive comment to your child, make a check mark in the positive comment column; negative comments are recorded in the negative comment column. If you use the paper and pencil method to record your comments, don't worry about the neutral column. It will just take up unnecessary time.

Here are some guidelines for helping you to judge your comments:

Positive Comments.   Did I:

1. use a positive greeting such as "hi" or "hello, honey"?
2. ask my child to do something rather than demand?
3. compliment my child on his behavior?
4. laugh with rather than at my child?
5. accept and praise my child rather than criticize?
6. pay positive attention to something my child was doing rather than ignore him or critize him?
7. thank my child for doing something for me?
8. say something affectionate such as "I love you"?
9. answer his questions in a positive way rather than putting him off?
10. take time to listen to him?
11. ask my child's opinion?

Negative Comments.   Did I:

1. say "no," "don't," or "stop that"?
2. criticize my child ("Don't do it that way." "That's not right")?
3. tell my child to leave me alone?
4. make a negative personal evaluation of my child ("You're dumb")?
5. demand rather than ask my child to do something?
6. use a negative greeting such as "Where have you been? I've been looking for you for the last half hour"?

7. tell my child he was doing something wrong rather than showing him the correct way to do it?

8. put him off by saying "in a minute" when he asked me something?

9. speak too quickly or loudly to my child in an attempt to "get rid of him" more quickly?

Neutral Comments.　Score as neutral any comments that do not include one of the above concepts and, in addition, score as neutral any comments on the weather, the house, etc., that are not evaluative of the child's behavior. If there are intervals when you have not spoken, include a score in the neutral column.

The above lists are not all-inclusive, but are intended to act as guidelines for your evaluation of your talk behavior. You will have to use your best judgment on many of the things you say, but try to be as objective as possible.

Evaluating Your Records

It would be highly unlikely and probably undesirable if you scored all your talk interactions as either positive or negative. Sometimes we are positive and other times we are negative. The best way to evaluate your records is in terms of the number of positive scores in relation to the negative scores. Are you more positive (more positive scores) or more negative? All other things considered, the greater the proportion of positive interaction scores, the more positive and supporting you are as a parent. A good guideline is: if you have three times more positive interactions than negative interactions, you are doing a pretty good job of being positive in your talk interactions with your children. If, however, you tend to be more negative than positive you might wish to consider the effects your being negative is having on your children. You probably aren't getting your children to behave as well as you would like (that's why you are being negative) and should consider changing your approach. I'll describe ways in which you can be more positive in your verbal interactions with your children. Try them and it's likely that your verbal relationship with your children will improve; but don't expect the improvement to occur overnight. Both you and your children have developed habits that will take a while to change, but change they will if you give it an honest try. You might even bring the children into your program of self-improvement. Ask them what they like and dislike about what you say to them. They might give you some insight into how they perceive what you say. You might even find that having the children help record your behavior will improve your relationship with each other.

EVALUATING BEHAVIOR
RATHER THAN THE CHILD

Experts agree that one of the most important things to consider when you are trying to change your child's behavior is evaluating the child's behavior rather than the child as a person. Look at the difference in what is said to a child in the following situations. An older child has just taken a toy away from his younger sister and the baby sister started crying. One parent might say, "Johnny, you bad boy, give that toy back to your sister." Another parent in the same situation might say, "Johnny, it's not nice to take things from someone when they are playing with them. Please give the toy back to your sister. You can play with it when she is finished, or ask her if you can play together." What is the difference in what is communicated to the child? In the first case, the parent is making an evaluation of the child as a person: the child is a bad boy. In the second situation the parent comments on the specific behavior (taking the toy) and says that the behavior is not proper—but the child is not evaluated. Is this difference important or superficial? I think it is important for several reasons. First, it is probably not true that the child is a bad boy. What is true is that the child sometimes does specific things that aren't appropriate, but he also does things that we like. The fact that someone occasionally does something that is not desirable does not mean that he has less worth as a person.

This is a philosophical argument for evaluating the behavior rather than the person, but there is another important psychological reason for focusing on the behavior rather than the person's worth. A child's self-concept or self-esteem is very much dependent upon what others say about him and to him. If a child is told that he is a good boy and given warm confirmation of this, he will grow up thinking well of himself. If, on the other hand, he told that he is bad, dumb, or not nice, he will say and think these things about himself.

s and Honesty in Talking to a Child

are the effects of a parent's lying to a child? Sometimes there
fect when the child either does not know that the parent lied or
he child does not understand that he was told a lie.

st children have great respect for their parents. They feel their
nts can't do wrong. Because of this, children will refuse to believe
r parents lied. It is because of this trust that lying, when found out,
be shattering to the child. When the child is aware of a lie, it can
eply affect the relationship between the parent and child. Let's look
a simple and seemingly harmless case of unintentional lying. A child
s doing something that annoys the parent and the parent says, "If you
don't stop doing that I'm going to send you to your room." The child
continues to misbehave and, after several more threats, the parent
does nothing, but only says to himself, "What can you do with a kid
like that?" In a sense, the parent has lied to the child and must suffer
the consequences. The parent told the child that the child's behavior,
if continued, would be punished. But it wasn't. When this happens
frequently, the child will disregard the parent's threats and continue to
engage in the behavior. In this example we can see that even an
unintentional form of lying will have consequences for the parent-
child relationship. The child ignores the parents, and the parent
becomes frustrated with the child. If this situation continues, severe
problems in the parent-child relationship can occur.

A similar type of lying is when the parent promises the child a
reward for being good and then fails to deliver the reward. Simply
put, in both this case and the case of the parent who threatened
punishment but didn't follow through, the child is learning not to
trust what the parent says. The consequence of this breakdown in trust
is that the parent will have less control over the child and may have to
resort to more extreme forms of control, such as physical punishment.

Although most parents don't plan to lie to their children, they can
get caught in a trap of unintentionally being dishonest. This occurs
when, in the best interests of our children, we tell them one thing and
then behave in a contrary way. For example, we tell our children that
it is not nice to hit smaller children—and yet we spank our children.
The parent might perceive a difference in the circumstances, but does
the child? To the child our behavior may be seen as hypocritical. What
effect does this have on the child? Several studies of children's help-

His behavior will also be affecte~~~
is stupid will be less willing to try ~~~
of an intellectual nature. He will, in ~~~
Robert Rosenthal, a psychologist ~~~
carefully, refers to it as a *self-fulfillin~~~*
become what we keep telling him he is ~~~
the extent prophesies can affect behavior, ~~~
we can have different effects on a child's e~~~
and goodness by saying different things to hi~~~
negative ways, he will have negative feelings ~~~
evaluations will produce positive feelings about h~~~

How one person is evaluated by another make~~~
ference in the relationship between the two people. ~~~
generally agree that a close involvement between two ~~~
tant for one to be able to help another. The necessary in~~~
occur when the helping person is willing to accept the ~~~
helped as a person. The helper may not like some of the ~~~
other person is doing and will often tell him so. But he is car~~~
the person being helped know that it is the behavior being ev~~~
not the person. Carl Rogers, one of the best-known psychother~~~
refers to this as having *unconditional positive regard* for the pe~~~
you are trying to help. You try to accept the person's worth regardl~~~
of what he does. You also try to help the person find better ways o~~~
doing things so that he not only is evaluated positively as a person, but ~~~
his behavior can also be evaluated positively.

Since much of what good parents try to do with their children is
similar to what a good psychotherapist does, the parent should also
try to learn to show unconditional positive regard for his children.
Again, this doesn't mean the parent should approve of his child's inappropriate behavior, but he should communicate to the child the
feeling "I like you, and will continue to like you, but I don't like some
of your behaviors and I will try to help you learn better ways of dealing with your world."

Another reason for evaluating behavior rather than the person is
that we are more likely to give the child precise feedback about what
we like and dislike. Saying "I don't like the way you hit your sister"
communicates much more than saying "You are a bad boy." Both the
parent and child know what behavior is of concern and should be
changed.

giving behavior have shown that children will not be helpful to others if they have been told by an adult to help and yet have observed the same adult act in a nonhelpful way. The child may adopt the adult's talking behavior and *say* that it is nice to help others, but he will behave as the adult does and not help others. The adult's lack of consistency is carried over to the child. Typically, the child does *not* obey the parent's rule of "Do as I say, not as I do."

If we want our verbal or talk behavior to control or influence the child's behavior, then it is necessary that we be consistent. If we want to have our children behave in a particular way, it is not enough to just tell them. We must act consistently with our verbal behavior. This is especially important when it comes to using words of affection with children. Parents, after they have just punished a child, often feel guilty about their actions and try "to make it up to the child" by telling him that they are sorry, that they really love the child. Look at the conflicting information that is given to the child. At first, the parent punishes and often says things like "You are a mean, terrible boy," and later, because of the guilt, says, "I love you." This discrepant information can be confusing to a child.

The solution to this situation is to let the child know—in other circumstances—that he is loved, but when you punish your child make sure you are correct in punishing. If you are, the child should be aware that you disapprove of his particular behavior but not of him as a person. If you feel you were correct in punishing the child, there is no reason for you to feel guilty and to apologize to the child and tell him you love him. Your previous behavior should have communicated your love. Statements of love that occur only because of guilt can also be interpreted by the child as hypocritical.

WHAT IS THERE TO TALK ABOUT?

How can we use talking to establish a better relationship and to help direct the behavior of our children? The first thing to keep in mind is that not all of our talk should be intentionally designed to direct the child's behavior. Talking should be fun and enjoyable for both parent and child. Parents and children should talk often and about many things, not just problems. Talking between parent and child can accomplish many things: it can be used to teach the child how to interact with his world, it can be used to learn more about the child's world, and it can be just for fun.

When Should Parent and Child Talk?

Often we find time to talk to our children only when there is a problem. This kind of problem-solving talk, although very important, usually occurs at times of stress. Either the child has a problem he wishes the parent to help solve or the parent has a problem with the child that the parent wants to solve. In either case there is a certain amount of tension in the situation and the talk is geared to solving the problem. Talking just for the fun of it or talk that is for the purpose of getting to know one another probably should not occur when tension is high. For example, if a parent wants to understand why his child did something surprising, but not a behavior that should be punished, this talk should not occur when the parent is upset or immediately following the child's behavior. In the past when the parent has talked to the child following similar actions, it was usually to reprimand the child. The child may carry the feelings that he is going to be reprimanded into the new situation. Later, when tension is lower and everyone has calmed down, the child is less likely to be defensive and anxious when talking about his behavior. In this more relaxed situation, both the parent and child are likely to get more out of talking. The parent will seem less harsh and not so disciplining, the child will be less anxious, and both will be more open and honest in their conversation. If, however, the child's behavior should be punished, then punish immediately. Later you can talk to the child about his behavior.

A parent should make free time to talk to his children. It shouldn't necessarily be an appointed time, but time should be available to the child. When you do find time to talk, don't talk to your child, talk with him. Give the child a chance to say what is on his mind.

EXAMPLE 2.1

A Child's Resistance to Temptation

A child sees an attractive toy and no one is around. Will the child take the toy? Or will he resist the temptation to take something that is not his? Whether a child will give in to his desires to take something that is not his depends in part on the way he has been taught to resist temptation. What is the best method of teaching a child to resist temptation? Should he be punished when he takes things that don't belong to him? Or should a parent seek to explain to the child the moral and rational reasons for not taking things? An interesting research study designed to provide some information on this problem showed that punishment might be less effective than a more rational approach.

The children in this study were placed in a situation where they could choose either an attractive toy or an unattractive toy. When some of the children chose the attractive toy they were told, "No! That's wrong. You must not choose that toy." Other children were told, "Those toys are for someone else. You've chosen the wrong toy." The first group of children were verbally punished, the second group were given a reason why they should choose another toy. The children who were given a reason chose the attractive toy far less often than the children who were verbally punished.

The fact that a child who is given a reason for not engaging in a particular behavior might resist temptation better than a child who was punished might not come as a surprise. But what might be surprising is that the children who were given reasons for their behavior tended to resist temptation much better when they were tested again two weeks later. Not only was reasoning with a child more effective the first time the child was placed in the temptation situation, but he was more likely to resist temptation at a later time.

From J. J. Leizer and R. W. Rogers, Effects of Method of Discipline, Timing of Punishment, and Timing of Testing on Resistance to Temptation. *Child Development,* 1974, vol. 45, pp. 790–793.

EXERCISE

How much time do you spend talking with your children? Are you like many parents who rarely ever spend time talking with their children? Or do you spend a fair amount of time talking with your child? Notice, I've used the concept "talking with" your child rather than "talking to" your child. Many parents "talk to" their children, and such conversation is often oneway— the parent does all the talking. There are several ways you can determine if you have been talking *with* your child rather than *to* your child. The first method, which is an indirect method of determining the form of verbal interaction between you and your child, is to try to think of as many things as possible that your child told you yesterday. Before reading further, get a pencil and paper and write down as many different things as you can remember. How many did you write down? Quite a few? Or hardly any at all? Now, using the following cues, try to write down some more:

1. Did your child mention anything to you about school? What subjects? Did he mention his teacher? His friends? Did he mention pleasant things? Unpleasant things?

2. What did your child do after school (or during the afternoon, if he is not in school)? Did he play with his friends? With whom did he play? What did they play?

3. Did your child say that he had a good night's sleep? Did he dream? Did he mention upcoming events? Did he enjoy his meals?

With these prompts you've probably added more things to your list. Do you think you spent enough time talking with him? It is difficult to decide how much is enough. Some children are not as talkative as others and on some days there is not as much to talk about. If you feel that you've been able to write down an adequate number of things which you and your child talked about, then you are probably spending a proper amount of time talking with your children. If, however, you feel a pang of guilt because you haven't been able to write down as many things as you feel is adequate, then you might wish to spend more time talking with your children.

A second and more direct method of determining how much time you spend talking with your child is to actually record the amount of time you and your children spend talking. Again, you will have to determine how much time is adequate and if you are spending this amount of time with your children.

I'd like to suggest that all parents could get to know their children better by spending more time talking with them. One way to encourage talking is to restrict the amount of time you watch television and to spend it with one another. There are a number of fun games—cards, checkers, and so on—that can be played to "break the ice" and encourage conversation.

3

Talking With Your Children: Helping To Solve Problems

If your child has engaged in a behavior that is inappropriate and stems from either lack of information or incorrect information, you can often help clarify the problem and prevent future occurrences of the behavior by talking to the child. During the conversation you should be concerned with trying to find out why the child did the behavior and to provide him with correct information. Knowledge of factors leading to the behavior will often point to the best way of solving the problem. Sometimes the problem can be solved by giving the child information that he previously did not possess. Other times it is necessary to correct the erroneous information he possesses.

When determining the factors producing the child's behavior, you should look to several sources: what happened prior to the child's behavior, what was happening at the time of the child's behavior, what happened to the child as a consequence of his behavior, and what were his feelings about his behavior.

Let's look at an imaginary conversation between a boy and his father. The boy had triggered off a fire alarm when there wasn't a fire.

When the firemen arrived, the child was still at the alarm box. The firemen then reprimanded the child and took him home to his parents. This conversation takes place after the firemen had left.

Father: Why did you do it, son?

Child: Johnny (*an older boy who lives down the street*) told me to.

Father: Where was Johnny when the firemen came?

Child: He said he had to go home, but I should stay and see what happened.

Father: Do you think it was right to pull the alarm?

Child: I wasn't going to, but Johnny said I was a sissy. I didn't think it would make anyone mad. Johnny said I could be his friend if I did.

Father: Sometimes we do things that we really don't want to do because someone else tells us to. Did you want to pull the alarm?

Child: Johnny said it would be cool.

Father: Do you think it is cool that you are in trouble with the firemen?

Child: No. I don't want them to be mad at me.

Father: What do you think Johnny thinks now?

Child: I don't know.

Father: Do you think Johnny might be laughing because he tricked you?

Child: (*after thinking for a minute*) Yes. He didn't get in trouble. I did.

Father: That's right. Do you think a friend would pull a trick on you like that?

Child: No. I don't think it was very nice of Johnny.

Father: Son, I'm unhappy that you let Johnny talk you into pulling the alarm, but I'm glad that you were honest and told me about it.

Child: Next time I won't do it if someone tells me to.

It is hoped the father would continue his conversation with his child and help the child understand that he shouldn't engage in behaviors that he feels are wrong just to please someone else. If the father handles the situation carefully, he can help the child understand the reasons he engaged in the behavior and the consequences of the behavior.

The conversation between the father and his child contain several good features. Notice that the father did not try to degrade his son. He explained to the child that he was unhappy with the child's action, but he did not try to make the child feel he was stupid or bad. Another nice feature is that the father was careful to reward the child's honesty, but not to reward the child's behavior. This is important. If we want our children to talk to us so that we might be able to help them behave in more appropriate ways, we must be careful to encourage their honest talking. This can be done without approving their behavior.

HOW TO ASK QUESTIONS

When we talk to our children and try to understand their behavior, it is important that we try to create a questioning atmosphere that will increase the child's honesty.

How do most parents question their children about some possible misdeed? Don't they direct the questions to the child in an accusative way, as if the child is already guilty? It only makes sense that a child who feels he has already been convicted tries every possible way of getting out of the situation, including lying. When a parent accuses, it is unlikely he will discover why the child did what he did. If, on the other hand, the parent tries to find out what happened and leaves the question of guilt aside for the moment, he is more likely to get the child to tell what really happened. Rather than beginning the questioning with accusations such as "That was really stupid, your turning on that alarm," or "My God, don't you know better than to do something stupid like that," a parent should begin with *problem-solving questions*. Problem-solving questions should take the form of "What were you doing when the behavior occurred, before the behavior occurred, and after the behavior occurred." Other problem-solving questions include "What do you think you did?" "How do you feel about it?" and "What do you think are the effects of your actions?"

The first set of questions tries to identify the situation: What led up to the behavior? What was the situation when the behavior occurred? What were the immediate consequences of the behavior? The second set of questions is directed to the feelings of the child at the time of the behavior and his knowledge of the consequences of his behavior. This kind of questioning can produce more information than can questions that begin with an assumption of guilt. The parent may find out that the child was unaware of the wrongness of his behavior, that the behavior was an accident, or that the behavior was premeditated and intended to do harm. If the latter is true, the questions help the parent discover why the child intentionally engaged in the behavior.

The structure of the question asked by the parent will determine the type of answer he receives. Questions can be broadly thought of as either open-ended questions or closed-ended questions. *Open-ended questions* do not require a definite, specific answer and are often used when the parent is first questioning the child. This can be useful in finding out a child's knowledge and feeling about what was done without necessarily implicating the child as the villain. Open-ended questions take the form of "What might have happened if . . ." or "Why do you think. . . ." In the example of the child who pulled the fire alarm, the father might have asked the child, "Why do you think the firemen were mad?" This question would not have accused the child of a wrongdoing, but would have let the father find out if the child was aware of the problems to the fire department when false alarms are turned in.

The second type of question—the *closed-ended question*—is more specific and asks for a specific answer. For example, when the father found that the child pulled the alarm after being told to do so by an older boy, the father asked a closed-ended question, "Where was Johnny when the firemen came?" This question demanded a specific answer. Closed-ended questions require specific answers; they more precisely define the situations and the causes of the behavior. Closed-ended questions are best asked once a parent has a general idea of why the child misbehaved; they are intended to clarify the problem and the solution.

Finally, the tone of the questions can either put the child at ease or put him on the defensive. A parent may carefully phrase his questions, yet his tone of voice implies he feels the child is guilty. This is done by talking too loudly, too rapidly, or by not allowing the child to speak. In other words, the question is not really intended to gather information, but to chastise the child. A question of this sort would be "Why do you think the firemen were mad? Don't you know it's wrong to pull the alarm?" These questions singly might get at the information the parent wants, but the way it is asked may make the child feel he is guilty and that he has no possible explanation. How will the child react? Probably defensively, cutting off the channels of communication.

As the parent identifies the circumstances and reasons for his child's behavior, he should consider ways of correcting the problem. The problem might be best corrected by giving the child information he didn't possess, the child might be punished, the parent might refuse to let him interact with certain of his friends, or the parent might wish to get help from a teacher or professional counselor.

HELPING A CHILD
SOLVE HIS SOCIAL PROBLEMS

We've discussed how to talk to a child when it's presumed he has engaged in some misbehavior but we are uncertain what motivated his behavior. We have discussed ways of finding out why the child misbehaved so we can make fair decisions about the consequences of his behavior. In this section, I will outline ways of talking to the child when he has not engaged in any wrongdoing, but has a problem he needs to solve. There are two levels at which the parent can help in solving a child's problem. Each successive level will require the parent to take a more directive role. The level of help provided by the parent will depend upon the nature of the problem, the child's concern about the problem, and the parent's evaluation of the child's ability to solve the problem.

Accepting the Child's Problem

The first level of parental help seems the simplest, yet in many ways can be the most difficult. This occurs when the child has a problem that is beyond his or your powers to solve. For example, how might a parent help a child when the child is told by older children that they do not want to play with him? We could tell the child that older children prefer to play with children their own age, but this still doesn't remove the child's hurt of being rejected. At best, in this situation, we can help the child to accept the situation. To do this, we must be willing to accept the child's hurt and not to dismiss his problems lightly. I've heard parents in this kind of situation say, "You think you have problems? You don't know what problems are. Wait until you're my age, then you'll really understand what it means to have problems." This is not a good way of handling the child's concern. First of all, to the child, his problems are every bit as serious and profound as your problems are to you. Secondly, this kind of answer is an excuse not to help the child deal with his problem. Finally, this response has the effect of creating concern about the depth of future problems. An analogous situation might be a woman who is in labor and hears another woman screaming about her pain. The first woman thinks,

"Wow, my pain is very bad but it must get worse; listen to that woman scream." The fact might be that both are experiencing equal pain, but one yells and the other does not. The one who does not yell, however, is getting a distorted picture of the reality of the situation.

Problems at any point in life are important and profound to the person who has them regardless of how we as outsiders evaluate the problem. If we are interested in trying to help, we should try to recognize that, for the child, his problem is important.

How can a parent go about accepting his child's problem and in turn help the child to accept the problem and the fact that little can be done to correct the situation? Maybe an example would help illustrate what a parent can do. Using the example of a child who has been rejected by older children, let's construct a way in which a parent might react.

Child: I hate Paul and Tom. They won't let me play with them.

Parent: It's kind of tough when someone says you can't play with them, isn't it?

Child: Yes, I don't like them anymore. They're not nice.

Parent: I can understand that you feel bad. Why do you think they don't want to play with you?

Child: They said I was too little. I'm not; they're just dumb.

Parent: Do you ever feel that you don't want your little brother to play with you?

Child: Sometimes. He messes up my toys and cries when I tell him how to play.

Parent: Maybe the older boys think you can't play their games as well as they do. Do you think so?

We'll leave this conversation unresolved and look at what the parent was trying to do. The parent understood that older children often do not like younger children tagging along. The parent also understood that his child was distressed by being rejected by the older boys. This is a necessary first step: the parent must empathize with the child's feelings and, because of his greater experience, empathize with the feelings of the older children. The parent's empathy will allow him to accept the child's feeling and possibly help the child understand the situation. It may very well be that the best the parent can do is to "lay the facts out" for the child in as understanding way as possible and let the child take what he will. This might involve letting the child know that you understand how he feels and try, possibly by analogy, to explain why the older children might have behaved as they did. The analogy is most effective if it can be made to be similar to an experience of the child's. In this case, the parent tried to show his child that he often had similar feelings about having his little brother play with him.

In the above example, there was little the parent could do but accept the child's hurt as real and try to reduce it by explaining the reality of the situation. If handled carefully and empathically, this treatment can help ease the child's hurt and help him understand why the older boys rejected him.

Accepting and Directing

Not every problem your child has with his social environment is unsolvable. Sometimes the parent, because of his greater experience and understanding of social dynamics, can help his child solve the problem. One way this can be done is by trying to understand the way the child feels about the problem and help him come to a solution. Helping the child come to his own solutions can be important; your solutions might not be right for your child and his situation.

One way to help the child make the best decision on how to handle his problem has been suggested by Dr. Jan Roosa. His system is designed for the parent or some other helping person to help the child decide what choices are open to him and the possible consequences of his actions. The system is called SOCS (*S*ituation, *O*ptions, *C*onsequences, and *S*imulation) and is basically a framework for helping people learn to more effectively manage their social environment.

Consider, for example, a child who is upset because one of his schoolmates has been spreading lies about him. How could the child best handle this problem? The child, because he is upset and because he isn't sure what to do, comes to his parents for direction.

The first thing the parent could do is to help the child formulate the problem—or, as it is termed in Roosa's framework, the *situation*. Let's suppose that the child has defined the situation as follows: his schoolmate has been telling lies about him and his friends have been teasing him and not playing with him—pretty serious problem for a young child.

Now, what are the options available to the child? This is the second part of the program. Let's imagine that, with the help of the parents, the child has decided that the following options are open to him:

1. He could fight the child who is telling the lies about him.
2. He could talk to his teacher and explain the problem and have her talk to the other children.
3. He could have his parents phone the parents of the child telling the lies and have them talk to their child.
4. He could tell lies about the child to get even.
5. He could confront the child directly and try to find out why he was telling the lies.
6. He could stay home from school so he wouldn't have to listen to his friends tease him.
7. He could try to talk to his friends and explain that the other child was lying.
8. He could fight with his friends each time they teased him.
9. He could just ignore the teasing and hope it would stop.

There are other options that are available, of course, but let's suppose these are the ones that the child, with the help of his parents, listed. The next thing the parents would try to help the child decide is the possible consequence of each of these options. Again they would be listed and the benefit of each considered. Suppose the child listed the following consequences. These are not necessarily the consequences to any one of the options, but what an action on his part might cause.

1. The other child might tell the teacher he is picking on him and get him in trouble.
2. The teacher could talk to the children explaining that it is not nice to tease their friends.
3. The children might call him a tattletale and tease him more.
4. The parents of the other child might tell their child to stop lying and apologize.
5. The other child might tell his friends that the boy is a cry baby.
6. The other children might not believe his lies about the other child and call him a liar.
7. He wouldn't feel good about telling lies, especially when he can see how bad lies have made him feel.
8. If he confronted the child, the child might not talk to him.

9. The other child might, if confronted, see that it is not nice to tell lies and stop lying.
10. If he stayed home from school, he would get behind his classmates and have trouble catching up.

The list illustrates the process the parent and child would go through when trying to decide which option is the best. The best option would be the one that had the best chance of solving the problem without creating other unnecessary problems.

The last stage is the simulation of the options and their consequences. Here the parent and child might role-play each of the options the child thinks might help solve the problem. For example, the parent might pretend he was the other child and role-play the various ways the other child might react to confrontation (assuming confrontation is one of the options considered by the child). Role-playing the situation will help expose the child to the possible reactions and give him experience in handling the reactions.

Compare the use of SOCS with a parent who just tells the child what to do. Suppose the parent's solution is "Tell the child that it's not nice to tell lies and that if he doesn't stop, you will tell the teacher." Although this solution might be the same as the child decides upon using SOCS, notice the differences. First, the child may have no idea as to how the other child will react (consequences), nor may he have the confidence to confront the child which he might have after practicing (simulation). In addition, the SOCS program will help teach the child how to evaluate new problems in the future. He will learn how to consider the options available to him and the possible consequences of each option.

Not all problems your child has with his social environment will require the elaborate consideration involved in SOCS. Sometimes simply asking the child what he thinks he should do is adequate. The child may have carefully thought about the problem and decided upon a course of action that is reasonable. Other times you may wish to tell the child what you think is the best solution. This might happen when the situation is very unusual and the child is unlikely to know how to act. For example, if the child is meeting a business associate of yours for the first time and you want the child to leave the room after the introductions, you might just tell him.

Talking with your child is effective for solving problems for several reasons. First, because you have more experience dealing with problems, the child has an "expert" who can provide information. This additional, and often superior, reservoir of knowledge increases the possible options available to the child. A second reason is that you might reduce the child's emotional upset produced by things that he either doesn't understand or that he is not sure how to deal with. Sometimes when an understanding parent talks to his child, the hurt or anger the child felt is reduced. When the child is less upset the problems he has may seem far less important. A third reason is that the parent can help motivate the child to engage in behaviors that solve the problem. Take, for example, a child who has broken a neighbor's window, but the neighbor doesn't know who did it. The child might be very upset and know he should apologize, but is afraid to. Together the parent and child may decide that the neighbor will be angry, but probably won't harm the child if he apologizes. The parent might then offer to accompany the child to the neighbor's place. In this situation the child needed an understanding parent who would not only help the child decide upon the correct course of action, but also someone who could motivate him.

Sometimes, talking to the child is not enough to correct the problem. In these cases, the parent should structure a program of change that will help the child improve his behavior. To do this he will have to combine talking with some of the other procedures described in other chapters.

EXAMPLE 3.1

Insight as an Aid to Learning

Helping a child understand his problem is often a very important first step in order for learning to take place. Although research has shown that it is not absolutely necessary for a child to understand his problem for learning to take place, the research is equally clear that understanding the problem greatly facilitates the learning of new behaviors. Insight or an understanding of the problem can be important even when working with young children. This was demonstrated by Drs. Don Peterson and Perry London. A three-year-old boy was brought to these psychologists by his parents because he was having severe problems with his bowel movements. The child would generally go about five days between bowel movements, and when he finally did eliminate it was very painful. The parents had tried laxatives prescribed by the child's doctor, but with little success.

The treatment program used by Peterson and London combined telling the child why he had problems eliminating (insight) and the use of rewards for successful bowel movements. The "insight" portion of the treatment consisted of telling the child how happy it would make everyone if he would have normal bowel movements and that the bowel movements hurt because he didn't go often enough. These messages were repeated over and over to the child in a slow, chanting sort of way. After the first session of insight therapy the child went home and had a successful bowel movement. The boy's happy parents rewarded the child with a popsicle. The child did not have another bowel movement until following the next insight therapy session. Thereafter, the child had normal, daily bowel movements which were rewarded by the parents with praise and popsicles.

Peterson and London conclude that the insight therapy, although possibly not necessary, greatly facilitated teaching the child to have normal bowel movements.

From D. R. Peterson and P. London, A Role for Cognition in the Behavioral Treatment of a Child's Eliminative Disturbance. In Ullman, L. P., and Krasner, L. (Eds.), *Case Studies in Behavior Modification.* New York: Holt, Rinehart and Winston, 1965. Pp. 289–294.

EXAMPLE 3.2

The Idealized Self-Image: A Method of Teaching Confidence

Sometimes when a child is feeling "low" and having difficulty interacting with others his parents can help out by aiding the child understand what he wants to do and how to do it. One method for doing this was suggested by Dr. Dorothy Suskind. She recommended that such *confidence training* proceed as follows:

The parent has the child imagine an *Idealized self-image* (ISI) that he can reasonably attain in a short period of time. This ISI should not be beyond the child's capability, but should be one which he can accomplish if he exerts himself. For example, a child who is feeling "low" because he didn't make the Little League baseball team might be encouraged to think of himself in training for next year and that he is going to learn to bat and throw better.

Next, the parent encourages the child to describe his ISI. The description should include those characteristics the child wants to attain. This will allow the parent to help the child make realistic appraisals of himself and to guide him in the next steps. For example, it would be foolish for a parent to encourage his child to adopt an ISI of being the best pitcher in the Little League if the child only has limited potential. The parent should encourage the child to adopt a more realistic ISI.

Next, the parent will encourage the child to consider what he must do to achieve his ISI. This step requires that the child not only describe the steps but engage in actions appropriate to reaching the goal. To help the child in this step the parent could remind the child of things he has done that resemble what he wants to do. For example, a parent might remind his child that he was really improving his hitting the baseball last year when he was practicing with his big brother. In addition, the parents should reward the child with praise for making efforts to improve and every time there is noticeable improvement in the child's performance.

Using this approach, the child will gain in confidence and be better prepared to accomplish his ends. This is especially likely because his parents have helped him select reasonable goals and have encouraged the child's work and progress toward these goals.

From Dorothy Suskind, The Idealized Self-Image (ISI): A New Technique in Confidence Training. *Behavior Therapy*, 1970, Vol. 1, pp. 538–541.

EXERCISE

Let's consider a situation that is common whenever young children get together. Let's imagine that we have a problem between two sisters, eight and five years old. The younger sister often pesters the older sister by following her around, and the older sister makes the younger feel bad by being rude to her. The result is that the parent gets complaints from both children. The older complains, "Mom, make Marcie leave me alone. She's bothering me." The younger sister argues, "But Mom, Donna said a nasty thing to me." Here we have a problem: How can we get the girls to be more cooperative and respectful of each other's feelings? How can we solve the problem? One way would be to talk to the girls and find out why they are behaving as they are. Let's approach the problem with a set of problem-solving questions. The questions are worded in a general form and can be used for a variety of problems. After reading the example you may wish to use the same questions to approach a problem of your own.

1. Under what circumstances does the problem seem to occur most often? In the above example, we might more specifically ask, "When does Marcie seem to bother her sister most often? Under what conditions does Donna seem to be most rude to Marcie?" By asking these general questions and observing the girls carefully, we might find out that Marcie "bothers" her sister most often when Donna has friends visiting or when Donna is playing with toys that Marcie especially likes. We may also find that Donna is most often rude if she has just been disciplined. These general questions help us define the problem or situation.

2. Given that the problem occurs most often in specific situations, how can I change the situations to reduce the likelihood that the problem will occur? More specifically, how can we change the conditions that produce the problem? In the above example we might suggest to Donna that it would cause fewer problems if, when she has her friends over or when she is playing with certain toys, she play with them in her room and close the door. Marcie could be told that when Donna's door is closed she is not to enter the room. For the other problem, Donna's rudeness to Marcie, we might wish to talk with Donna and explain that we have noticed that she is rude to her sister after she has

been disciplined. We could then talk to her about how it is unfair to take out her feelings on her sister. If the family situation is generally happy, this should help reduce Donna's rudeness to Marcie.

3. Given that changing the situation has lessened the problem, how can I make sure the problem does not return? Although changing the situation may have improved the problem, this is no guarantee that the problem will continue to remain solved. Sometimes we must do other things to maintain the improved state. One method is to praise the children for their improved way of acting. The praise can do two things: help maintain the improved behavior and provide you with more opportunities to talk with your children and find out if new problems are arising.

4. If changing the situation doesn't improve the problem, then what should be done? Basically, this is a backup plan. Sometimes our first attempts don't work, especially when they are simple changes of conditions, and we should be prepared to use other methods to produce the desired changes. The next chapters will give you ideas that you can use in your backup plan.

4

Punishment:
The First Line
Of Defense

I once asked a group of parents, "When do you punish your children and why?" The most common answer was that they punished when their children had repeatedly engaged in an inappropriate behavior. Before punishing, however, the parents said they generally tried talking to their children and explaining why they should stop misbehaving. If the child continued to engage in the inappropriate behavior, the parents usually punished the child with spankings or slaps.

From this discussion and other observations I'm convinced that most parents prefer not to use punishment, but use it when talking fails to change the child's behavior. This is especially true for parents of young children. As a child grows older and his parents continue to have difficulty controlling his behavior using reason and other verbal methods, parents often use punishment more and more. When a parent does begin to punish frequently, other ways of controlling the child's behavior occur less and less often. The parent no longer is willing to try to talk to the child about the misbehavior.

The frequent use of punishment is somewhat of a trap. A parent tries talking to his child, but fails to accomplish what he desires, so he punishes. Punishment often produces the desired change in the child's behavior—at least temporarily. Because punishment seems to work where other methods have failed, the parent uses it more and more frequently. This is the trap. Rather than trying to find other methods that are as effective as punishment, the parent uses what seems to work: punishment.

This presents an interesting paradox. Many parents who use punishment as their major method of controlling their child's behavior dislike using punishment because, they claim, it doesn't always accomplish what they want. It may stop the child from engaging in an inappropriate behavior for a short period of time, but the child often engages in the same behavior at some later time. Besides, many parents don't like what punishment does to their relationship with their children. The parent feels bad when he punishes and the child often becomes angry and remote.

If parents recognize that the effects of punishment are not always long-lasting and that punishment can sometimes undermine the relationship with their children, why do they continue to use it? There are at least two reasons: first, because it works better than some of the other, weak methods of discipline they are using; and secondly, because as children and as adults they have been taught to use punishment.

Punishment can be an important tool for teaching children, if used properly. It can, with proper usage, be effective and produce long-term effects. The problem is that punishment is often overused (to the exclusion of more positive methods) and used incorrectly. In this chapter we will look at why some parents overuse punishment, and how punishment can be used more properly and when punishment should be used.

LEARNING TO PUNISH

In Chapter 1 I showed that some parents are more likely to punish their children than are others. Why do some parents make extensive use of punishment and others only use punishment sparingly? There are probably a number of reasons, but two seem especially important for our discussion. Some parents punish their children because this is the way they were taught as children to interact with people. The second reason people punish is that their early personal experiences have taught them that this is one way of making people behave as they wish. In other words, people learn to punish because others have taught them to use punishment and because they have personally discovered that punishment can change the behavior of others.

Because these two concepts are important for understanding why some people frequently punish and others don't, let's look at each type of learning more closely.

As children, our parents taught us many things such as how to interact with others, the people we should like and dislike, and the way we should feel about many things. Often, because of these teachings, we continue to behave as adults in the ways taught by our parents. The same is true with our child-rearing patterns. If your parents were warm and loving, you are likely to be warm and loving as a parent. If your parents frequently used punishment as a teaching tool, you are likely to use punishment with your children. Drs. D. Gelfand and D. Hartmann, two child psychologists, and their colleagues have demonstrated this relationship between the methods adults use to teach children and the methods that children who observed the adults use to teach other children. Children who observed adult models using rewards also used rewards when they had an opportunity to teach another child. But if the adults they observed used punishment, so did the children.[1]

This was an important finding because it provided definite, scientific evidence that children will often adopt the methods of interacting with others—including peers—that their parents used. Parents do indeed affect the child's style of interacting with others.

Parents, of course, are not the only people who determine the child's style of interacting with others, but because of the parents' early influence, the basic pattern is probably established in the home. Whether the child will use punishment when he becomes an adult depends on how successful the use of punishment by the child is in controlling his environment. If the child finds that others give in to the punishing tactics he has learned, he will continue to use punishment. If he finds that punishment is successful only in certain situations, he will use punishment only in those situations. For example, if a child

[1]Gelfand, D.M., Hartmann, D.P., Lamb, A.K., Smith, C.L., Hahan, M.A., and Paul, S.C. The Effects of Adult Models and Described Alternatives on Children's Choice of Behavior Management Techniques. *Child Development,* 1974, Vol. 45, pp. 585-593.

finds that punishment is effective only with children smaller than himself, he will develop a pattern of behavior we might call bullying.

A second way a person learns to punish is through direct experience. A child, for example, who is being unpleasantly teased by a friend might find that he can reduce or eliminate the teasing by hitting his friend, thus punishing his friend for teasing. If the other child stops teasing, an important lesson has been learned: if somebody is doing something that makes me unhappy, I can stop them—and the unhappiness—by hitting them. The strategy works—at least for a while—so the child becomes more likely to use punishment.

We've seen that people learn to punish for two reasons: first, by observing others, especially parents, who use punishment when interacting with others. In this case, what the child learns is "This is the way people are to be treated. My mother and dad do it, so it must be ok." A child may not actually say these things, but his behavior indicates this is what he may have learned.

The second way in which a child learns to punish is through direct experience. He finds himself in an unpleasant situation and, sometimes intentionally and sometimes by accident, finds that if he punishes the person producing the unpleasantness, the unpleasantness stops. In this case, what is learned is "If someone causes me pain, I can eliminate that pain by punishing the person causing the pain." Generally speaking, both of these learning experiences are unfortunate. The child develops a style of living that is selfish: he is temporarily benefited by controlling his environment, but he will have learned little about using more positive ways of interacting with others. If successful, this style of interacting can persist into adulthood, and when the child becomes a parent, he may continue the pattern of using punishment and teach his children to use punishment.

There are other, less selfish reasons why people punish. These reasons typically center around the desire to prevent someone from doing something which will either harm himself or someone else. For example, a parent might find that the best way to keep a child from playing with an electrical outlet is to slap his hands. This is an example of when the use of punishment might be appropriate. If a parent uses punishment to prevent a child from engaging in behavior that will cause immediate harm to himself or someone or something else, then punishment might be appropriate.

But regardless of why punishment is used, one weakness with punishment as a teaching tool is that it only works to stop a child from engaging in certain behaviors, but it does not teach behaviors that are more appropriate. For this reason, punishment when it is not used to prevent a child from harming himself or something else might be used inappropriately. It does not teach new behavior. This is an important principle of punishment: *punishment, by itself, does not teach what should be done.* All that is taught is what *not* to do. If a child is not taught appropriate behaviors (what to do), he will either avoid that situation or continue to try new behaviors in that situation. Some of these behaviors might be appropriate and others inappropriate. If the parent simply punishes inappropriate behavior, the child may never develop the proper skills or behaviors in that situation.

WHAT IS PUNISHMENT?

Before we can adequately describe how to use punishment more effectively, we should talk about what punishment really is. There tends to be differences in what many people think punishment is and how professionals describe punishment. Let's look at two examples. One will fit the technical definition and you can see if you were correct.

For the first example, imagine a child who comes into the house with mud on his feet, tracks mud across the floor, and goes into his room where he takes off his muddy shoes. Fifteen minutes later, the mother notices the mud, goes into the child's room, spanks the child, and sends him outside. During this interactional episode the mother doesn't say why she is spanking the child.

Now, for the second example, imagine a child who reaches for an electrical cord which is plugged into a wall socket. When he does, the father slaps the child's hand and says, "Don't touch!" After three repetitions of this the child stops reaching for the electrical cord.

In an everyday concept of punishment both situations might be considered punishment. This is because many people confuse punishment with the act of hurting someone (or taking something away from a child). This isn't exactly correct, at least in the technical sense of punishment. *Punishment,* defined technically, is doing something to the child immediately following his behavior which reduces the likelihood that the child's behavior will be repeated. The actual thing done to the child can, and does, vary considerably, but what is important is the effect the consequence has on the future occurrences of the child's behavior. If the child readily repeats a behavior even though we spanked him the last time, then the spanking does not fit the technical definition of punishment.

Let's clarify the technical concept of punishment by reviewing the two examples. In the first example, the mother spanked the child and sent him outside. Was she using punishment according to our technical definition? No, but why not? Was it because she didn't tell the child why he was being spanked? Not really. Although some research has found that punishment is more effective (changes behavior more rapidly) when the child is told why he is being punished, other research has shown that it is not absolutely necessary for the child to know why he is being punished for his behavior to change. Then is the first example technically not punishment because of the fifteen-minute delay between the time the child tracked mud on the floor and when he was spanked? Again, that is not the reason. There is no doubt that punishment which immediately follows the child's behavior is more effective than punishment which is greatly delayed. But punishment, under certain circumstances, can be effective when there is a delay between the child's act and the punishment. The reason the first example cannot be strictly classified as punishment is that there is no indication that spanking the child and sending him outside had any effect on his future behavior. In other words, we don't know if the spanking had any effect on reducing the number of times the child came into the house with mud on his feet.

Let's take a look at the second example. This is a much better example of punishment. We can see that the spank on the hand and saying "Don't touch!" stopped the child from touching the electrical cord. In addition, two other aspects of the situation make this a better example of punishment: the hand spank followed the behavior (reaching) immediately, and the child was told what not to do ("Don't touch!).

Types of Punishment

Any of a number of things that a parent does to a child can act to punish the child's behavior. For example, if a child swears at his parents, the parents might spank the child, or the parent might send the child to his room. Both of these activities on the part of the parent are potential punishers. There are, in fact, three broad classes of punishment: physical punishment, removal of privileges, and verbal punishment. There are advantages and disadvantages with the use of each, and choice of one over the other (if punishment is the teaching strategy of choice) should be based on the merits of each.

Physical Punishment. Physical punishment is the most common form of intentional punishment used with young children. When we use physical punishment, we physically interact with our child, usually causing the child some pain. The most common forms of physical punishment are spanking, slapping, hitting, and shaking. The latter, shaking a child, at first glance seems less severe than the other forms of physical punishment. But is it? Recent finding by medical doctors have shown that whiplash effects are not uncommon following the shaking of a child. The whiplash can be severe enough to cause damage to the vertebrae of the neck. This example was included to indicate that physical punishment, although it generally produces changes in behavior more rapidly than other forms of punishment, should be used intelligently with full knowledge of the effects it will have on the child. Intelligent use of punishment does not occur when a parent uses physical punishment in a "fit of anger." A parent who is very angry should, for the sake of his child and his relationship with the child, consider the next form of punishment.

Removing Privileges. The second type of punishment is when we remove the child's privileges when he behaves inappropriately. Typically this takes two forms: (1) removing the child from a situation he is enjoying, such as sending a disruptive child to his room, and (2) taking something away from the child, such as his being able to watch television for the evening. Many parents who don't wish to use physical punishment prefer these forms of punishment. They seem less cruel—and they probably are, if used correctly.

A problem with using isolation, or removing a child from a situation he is enjoying, is that it is often done not to teach the child, but selfishly—to get the child out of the parent's hair. Let me give you an example of what I mean. A child is goofing off at the dinner table and the parent has repeatedly said, "If you don't eat, I'm going to send you to your room." The child continues to misbehave. Finally, the parent sends the child to his room. Is the parent punishing the child? As we've already learned, without more information it is impossible to tell, but my experience tells me that for many children, being sent to their room is not very punishing (especially if it follows repeated threats). Children would often rather be in their room where they can play with their toys than being at the table eating something they don't like. Thus, removing a child in these circumstances is not really punishment.

Another way that isolation is misused is the duration of the time used to punish the child. There is probably little advantage in removing the child from the table, for example, for more than ten to fifteen minutes. Longer durations probably are more effective for producing bad feelings than for effectively changing the child's behavior.

The effects of brief periods of isolation can be made to be very effective if when the child is released from isolation, he is made to correct the action that produced punishment. Correcting the action that produced punishment will be discussed later, but the logic is that many children would be willing to suffer brief privations to get out of doing some things they don't like. If a child's behavior was such that it should have been punished in the first place, then it is probably important enough to request the child to correct it after he has been removed from isolation.

In fact, having a child correct his inappropriate behavior might make punishment unnecessary. An alternative to punishing the child would be to allow him an opportunity to engage in the correct behavior and to repair the results of his misdeed. For example, a child who took a toy away from his younger brother might be given the option of returning the toy and apologizing to his younger brother or returning the toy and sitting on a chair in the kitchen for two minutes. Providing the child with an option can often reduce the child's anger produced by being punished. More importantly, it provides the child with an opportunity to practice a positive behavior. The use of positive practice as part of a punishment system has several desirable teaching features which will be discussed more fully in a later section.

If you do use isolation and remove the child from where his misbehavior occurred, where should you send him? Virtually anyplace can be used as long as it does not allow the child to do things that are more fun than what he was doing. If a child is sent to his room and he plays with his toys, then you are not punishing him. In fact, you may be teaching the child to misbehave just to be sent to his room. Many parents use the old-fashioned idea of having the child stand or sit in the corner of a room. This is as good a place as any, especially if the child is not there for more than a few minutes.

Removing the child from the situation where his inappropriate behavior occurred is to remove something from the child. This can take two forms. First we could, say, take a toy away from the child when he is mistreating it. This is similar in many respects to the use of isolation, but here, rather than removing the child, we remove what the child is engaged with. The second method is to remove some privilege which is unrelated to the behavior, but is desired by the child when he misbehaves. In this situation, we might, for example, not allow the child to watch television at night if he fights with his sister.

The various methods of removing privileges can be equally effective as punishers. The choice of one over the other will depend upon such things as circumstances, the age of the child, and the behavior to be punished. Isolation, for example, might be appropriate when the child's behavior disrupts others.

Verbal Punishment. The last category of punishment commonly used by parents is verbal punishment. Another, and probably a more correct, term for verbal punishment is *conditioned punishment,* which implies that the child has learned, or been conditioned, to associate what you say with some other type of punishment such as physical punishment. After several repetitions of your saying "Stop that!" and spanking the child, the statement alone will terminate the child's behavior. But because most conditioned punishers are verbal, we will retain the term *verbal punishment* for purposes of description.

I mentioned above, when discussing punishment, that physical punishment is the most common form of intentional punishment. Verbal punishment is the most common form of unintentional punishment. Several studies on how people talk to one another have found that we tend to say negative things much more often than positive things, especially to our children. These negative statements can, and often do, act to punish the behavior of others. There is a story that is passed around that I personally can't verify (but it sounds about right) that illustrates my point. A mother took her two-year-old daughter to their family doctor and asked the doctor, "Doctor, what can I do? My daughter is in a very negative stage. She is constantly saying 'no' and 'don't'." The wise doctor asked the mother if she frequently said "no" and don't" to her daughter. The mother said, "No," but was asked by the doctor to keep track of the number of times she said "no" and "don't" to her child. The next day the mother telephoned the doctor during the noon hour and said, "Doctor, I think I understand what you meant. It's only noon and I've already said 'no' 250 times."

The point of the story is that most of us are quite unaware of how often we use negative comments when interacting with others, especially our children. In addition, when we say negative things we often say things that will accomplish little more than hurting the child's feelings. Let's look at two examples where a parent uses verbal behavior to try to punish a child. One of the examples is obviously an example of poor usage of words to punish a child's behavior. See if you can tell which example makes best use of verbal punishment and why.

Example 1. A small child is chasing the family dog around the house and trying to hit the dog with a toy. The father sees the child and says, "Stop chasing the dog; you might hurt him. I don't like you doing that; it frightens the poor dog. If you keep chasing him, I'll take that toy away from you." The child stops and says, "Okay, Dad, I'll stop."

Example 2. Let's look at the same situation, handled differently. When the parent sees the child chasing the dog, he says, "Stop that, Johnny. You're a very bad boy. How many times do I have to tell you to stop chasing the dog. God, you're stupid." The child stops, puts his head down, and leaves the room.

Let's look at what happened in each situation. The first thing we notice is that both ways of handling the situation were effective in getting the child to stop chasing the dog. But in one case the parent's choice of words might have effects beyond just getting the child to stop doing the behavior. In the first example, the parent told the child to stop the behavior and why he should stop—the toy will be taken away. This additional information given to the child tells the child why this specific behavior is inappropriate and the consequences if he doesn't stop. There are no evaluations of the child's goodness. It is the behavior that the parent focuses on. What about the second example? Here the parent makes no mention of why the child should stop chasing the dog except that he is a *bad boy* and a *stupid boy*. The particular behavior is not the concern; it is the child's goodness. The parent is not condemning the specific act, but the child. Can these two styles of verbally punishing the child have different effects on the child? Probably. In the first case there would probably be little or no resentment or negative carryover that is of any importance. In the second example, however, the parent is telling the child more than to just stop chasing the dog. The parent is evaluating the child's goodness or personal worth. When this happens repeatedly, the child often begins to behave in accordance with how his parents evaluate him. If they continually tell the child he is stupid, then he will behave in stupid ways. What a child is and what he becomes is determined not only by what parents and others intentionally do to a child, but also what they do unintentionally. Parents of children who have more problem behaviors than most also had good intentions. Good intentions are not enough. A person must be aware of what effect his behavior might have on others. The use of criticism and other forms of personal condemnations are common when interacting with others because we often can't see their effects. Let me give you an example of what I mean. A child who was sent to a psychologist because of his frequent disruptive behavior was asked why he did things that made his parents mad. The child answered, in all seriousness, that he misbehaved because he was a bad boy. How did he know he was a bad boy? Because his parents told him so. He was fulfilling their prophesy: he was being bad. His parent could have just as easily told the child that his specific behaviors were inappropriate or bad, but still let the child know that he—the child—had personal worth and was loved by his parents.

So far we've discussed how a person might learn to use punishment, what is and what isn't punishment, and the common types of punishment. In the next chapter we will look at some situations where it might be appropriate to use punishment. I'm sure that you will be able to think of other situations where punishment might be the strategy of choice to use for teaching a child. I'm equally sure that you might be able to think of better ways to handle the situations I've described. What I'm going to present are general guidelines for when punishment might be used. Try to keep in mind while reading about these situations that it is generally possible to use more positive approaches whenever punishment is used. If you can use a positive approach in these situations, then do.

EXAMPLE 4.1

Isolation and Its Effects
on Other Children

Sometimes what a parent does to one child will have effects on other children in the home. This was demonstrated in a case study where a mother requested help with her three-year-old son, Teddy. Teddy was reported to whine and demand constant attention. In addition, Teddy hit other children, abused the family dog, screamed shrilly for long intervals, and generally engaged in disruptive behaviors. Teddy's mother was trained to react appropriately to Teddy's behavior. Whenever Teddy was engaging in disruptive behavior, a psychologist, who was helping Teddy's mother, would signal her to *ignore* Teddy. If Teddy was engaged in appropriate behaviors, the mother was signaled to *reward* Teddy with attention and praise. This was continued for several days. Because it is difficult (and sometimes inappropriate) to ignore all of a child's inappropriate activity, the psychologist had Teddy's mother try a new approach. Now, in addition to praising Teddy for appropriate behavior, Teddy's mother was asked to put Teddy on a chair in the hallway each time he engaged in one of the inappropriate behaviors.

The results were interesting. Rewards and ignoring had little effect on Teddy's behavior, but as soon as the mother started putting Teddy in the hall when he misbehaved, his rate of misbehavior decreased greatly and his rate of appropriate behavior increased. A second interesting finding is that the teaching program which was designed for Teddy also had a very positive effect on his five-year-old sister. Although the sister's behavior was not considered a problem, she would occasionally behave inappropriately. When the treatment program began for Teddy, his *sister's behavior was even better than before.* This effect might have been due to a number of factors: first, the mother was probably more effective with her children, and secondly, the praise and isolation Teddy received may have encouraged his sister to behave more appropriately. Whatever the reason, this example shows that more appropriate parenting methods can have wide-ranging implications for your interactions with your children.

From H. Laviguer, R. Peterson, J. G. Shoese, and L. Paterson, Behavioral Treatment in the Home: Effects on Untreated Sibling on Longer Follow Up. *Behavior Therapy*, 1973, Vol. 4, pp. 431–441.

EXERCISE

The purpose of this exercise is to help you determine if you are using punishment effectively. You earlier learned that there is a difference between just hurting (or yelling at) someone and punishing them for some specific behavior. To call what you do to your child *punishment*, it must reduce the occurrence of the behavior. Think of an example of behavior in which your child engages that you feel you have been punishing. Did you obtain the desired effect? Did the child stop engaging in the behavior? If the child did stop, then you were probably using punishment effectively; but if the behavior persisted, you were probably not using it as well as you might.

If the behavior did not change as you had hoped, ask yourself the following questions:

1. What did I do to the child that I thought would stop him from engaging in the behavior? The purpose of this question is to help you recognize the type of aversive stimuli you were using. Could what you did be best classified as a physical punisher? A privilege remover? Or a verbal punisher? If you are like most parents, you probably don't use verbal punishers as effectively as you

could. They are, at best, weak punishers, especially for young children. If you decide that you've been primarily using verbal punishers, you should consider one of the other two types.

2. If I used physical punishment, what kind of reaction did I get from the child? Sometimes when we spank our children we "pull our punches." In fact, the spank is nothing more than a token pat on the behind. This, unfortunately, is a very weak punisher for most children. After awhile they either don't respond to a mild form of physical punishment or they respond with defiance. Whichever they do, they are telling you that the punishment was probably not very effective and the behavior will occur again. If you feel that you should use punishment, but you don't want to really hurt your child (which is rather admirable), then you may wish to consider using a form of removing privileges.

3. If I removed a child's privileges, did I let him enter a situation that was more desirable than the situation that he was removed from? Although removing privileges is probably the most effective form of punishment for most parents, we do make one common mistake: we end up letting the child enter a more pleasant situation than he was removed from. For example, if you punish a child for playing too roughly with his toys by sending him to his room, you might be sending him to a place that was more enjoyable than the one he left. If privileges are to be removed, it is important that the child be restricted from other pleasant activities for the duration of the removal of the privilege.

4. Did I weaken the effects of my punishment by apologizing to the child or by showing guilt? Punishment should be intelligently used. That means, at least in part, that the child should be punished only if he was deserving the punishment. If he was, then there is no need to feel guilty and apologize to the child. If you do, then you may have weakened the effects of the punishment because the child might understand the apology as saying, "What you did was really not inappropriate. It was I who misbehaved."

5

Making Punishment Effective

As we have seen, many people use punishment improperly. When punishment is used badly, it often has little effect on the desired action—decreasing the behavior of concern. What does happen if punishment is used badly is an increase in negative feelings between parent and the child. A parent who uses punishment in improper ways can increase the emotional behavior of the punished child. If this happens, the problem is compounded: the parent improperly punishes his child, the child becomes emotional and says or does something that makes the parent punish the child again. Here we have the makings of a very unhappy relationship between parent and child. The child learns to dislike the parent, and the parent is at wits' end over his problem child. This situation is totally unnecessary and can often be prevented if the parent is aware of the effects his actions have on the behavior of his children.

WHEN IS PUNISHMENT EFFECTIVE
AND WHEN SHOULD IT BE USED?

Punishment does not have to produce bad side effects. It seems that emotional behavior occurs only when punishment is used as the primary way of teaching the child about his world. The proper use of punishment can be considered in two ways: the particular situation when a child's behavior needs to be decreased, and when punishment is used to supplement more positive teaching methods. These are not mutually exclusive conditions. In fact, punishment is most effective when combined with alternative strategies that are more positive.

When Rapid Behavior Change Is Necessary

The first condition where punishment might be the desired tool for teaching a child is when a rapid behavior change is necessary. Let's look at an example of a situation which demands rapid behavior change and punishment seems to be the appropriate tool. Suppose a mother just brought her new baby home from the hospital. Her three-year-old is very interested and wants to play with the baby. One time, she went into the bedroom and the three-year-old has accidently pulled a blanket over the baby's head while they were playing. This obviously can't be allowed to continue. What should the mother do? Punishment in the form of a firm slap on the wrist and a loud "no" would be very appropriate. Later, when the three-year-old has stopped crying or sulking, she might wish to talk to him about what he did and why she spanked him. If she did talk to her child, she shouldn't have apologized for her actions. She was in the right. A poorly formed apology might make the child feel the mother was wrong for what she did and that the behavior of putting the blanket over the baby's head was not all that bad.

Let's analyze this situation. Why was punishment appropriate? First, there was a need for rapid behavior change. Rapid behavior change is necessary when the child is engaging in a behavior that, if not immediately stopped and permanently discontinued, might cause harm either to the child or to someone else. Other, more positive procedures might work, but it is unlikely they will work with the speed and effectiveness of punishment. Punishment properly used can produce dramatic and rapid changes in behavior. That is one of the reasons people use it so frequently—it often works where other methods have failed. The person who uses it is rewarded by the child's change in behavior and is more likely to use it again.

Secondly, this was a situation where the message to be taught to the child was what not to do. In this case it was to not put the blanket over the baby's head. As a teaching device, punishment is only effective in teaching children what not to do. If the mother in this situation had wanted to teach the child other ways of playing with the baby, then a different approach would be necessary. Punishment cannot teach appropriate behaviors.

Using Punishment with Positive Alternatives

If in the above situation the mother wanted to teach her child to interact with the baby in positive, constructive ways, then she should use positive teaching methods. Several positive methods will be described in the following chapters, but for now let's briefly look at how punishment can be combined with a positive teaching method. The mother might want her three-year-old to stroke and kiss the baby, but not cover the baby's face, pinch, or hit the baby. How could she accomplish these ends with her three-year-old? The first thing she could do is tell her child which behaviors are ok and which behaviors are not ok. When the parent observes the child engaging in the forbidden behaviors, the child should be punished in one of the ways described earlier: physical punishment, withdrawal of privileges, or verbal punishment. Because of a three-year-old child's limited vocabulary, verbal punishment is probably not so good a choice as the other two. Verbal punishment becomes more effective as the child is older and after verbal punishment has been associated with either physical or removal-of-privilege punishment. In other words, the child must learn what is meant when the parent says "No!" The effectiveness of verbal punishment with younger children is because the parent usually yells and frightens the child. The actual words generally have little effect.

In addition to punishing the child for the behaviors which were deemed undesirable, parents should increase the behaviors that are desirable. How can they do that? There are several methods, but they all basically boil down to rewarding the child when he engages in the desired behaviors. In our example, whenever the mother saw her three-year-old kissing the baby, she could praise him by saying something like, "Isn't it nice that you love our baby so much. I think you are really nice, Can you help me give the baby a bath?" This attention from the mother is sure to increase the positive behavior of the three-year-old toward the baby.

What is the parent doing when punishing the child for the behaviors which might harm the baby and rewarding the child for his effectionate behavior? The parent is teaching the child to *discriminate* which behaviors are appropriate in certain situations. Pinching, smothering, and hitting are not appropriate and will be punished; affectionate behaviors are ok and will meet with the approval of the parents. The child is not only being taught what not to do, but the parent is making an effort to teach the desirable behaviors, a much better situation than when punishment alone is used. The child is not left to guess what should be done. He is told what will happen when he engages in either the appropriate or inappropriate behaviors, and when he does, the parent follows through with the promised consequences.

This positive and negative feedback will teach the child how to interact with his world and reduce the emotion of now knowing what to do or the emotion produced by the overuse of punishment.

MAKING PUNISHMENT EVEN MORE EFFECTIVE

We have seen that punishment can be an effective and desirable tool for changing a child's behavior when we need rapid behavioral changes and when punishment is combined with more positive methods. Now let's look at why punishment is an effective tool for changing behavior.

How often should we punish? How frequently should we punish? How soon after the child misbehaves should we punish? These are questions that must be answered before we can understand the effectiveness of punishment.

I think you will find that some of the things that make punishment most effective are either difficult for you to do or go against your moral fiber. If so, consider the effects that poorly used punishment has on the behavior of your child. Ask yourself what you want to accomplish when you punish your child. Do you want to be maximally effective in teaching your child not to do certain things, or are you willing to risk using a less effective approach? You'll probably decide that the answer to this problem depends upon the behavior you are punishing. If it is important that the child stop engaging in some behavior, you will probably want to use punishment in its most efficient way. If, however, the misbehavior is of less importance and only occurs infrequently, you may wish to use a less severe and less effective form of punishment. Whichever level of effectiveness you choose, keep in mind that combining punishment with positive parenting methods greatly improves the effectiveness over just using punishment.

How Soon After the Child Misbehaves Should He Be Punished?

We've already touched upon this question earlier, but I should spend some time giving the rationale behind the importance of punishing as soon after the behavior occurs as possible. What do we want to accomplish when we punish a child for some behavior? We want to make sure that he doesn't do that behavior again, at least in the circumstances where the behavior occurred this time. We don't want to confuse the child or develop hard feelings if these can be prevented. In other words, what we want to do is to teach the child something about how he should interact with his world and how to interact responsibly. To do this we must make sure that our behavior— the behavior of punishing—affects only the child's inappropriate behavior. Can this be done if we wait for a long period of time before punishing? Imagine this situation. A child does something that the child's mother thinks is inappropriate and deserving of punishment, but, for some reason, does not punish the child. She tells the child that when his father gets home, he will punish the child. Several hours later the father arrives home and is greeted by the child who might have forgotten all about his earlier misbehavior. The mother comes into the scene and tells the father to punish the child, which he does with a spanking. What is the father punishing? Possibly several things, and possibly not what the mother wanted punished. The father might be punishing (reducing the likelihood of) the child's greeting behavior. This is the behavior that occurred just prior to the child being punished. A general rule is that *punishment affects most those behaviors that occur immediately before the punishment.* This is especially true for younger children. As children grow older, the parent can describe the situation and help "bring to mind" the behavior being punished so that punishment will have more effect on the behavior of concern. But, regardless of the child's age, if the punishment does not occur soon after the misbehavior, other events will take place that will also be affected by the punishment.

It is not always possible to punish immediately after the child misbehaves. How can you get around this problem? One way is to use a procedure where the child loses privileges that are progressively more remote in time. For example, when a young child misbehaves, you might immediately restrict him from going outside and playing with his friends for five minutes. Later, when he misbehaves again, you may restrict his watching a favorite television show that is on in an hour. Each time you restrict his activities, it is important to tell him what is restricted, for how long the restriction is in force and when it comes time to restrict his activity, he should again be told why it is being restricted. When you talk to the child about his behavior and the restricted activity, you should try to be as matter of fact as possible: being mad or upset will not help the effectiveness of the punishment. All your emotional behavior will do is increase your negative feelings and make your child unnecessarily upset.

Essentially what you are doing when you progressively increase the time between the child's misbehavior and the punishment is to teach the child to tolerate the delay between his behavior and its consequences. This will help prevent the problem of punishment being associated with the wrong behavior. With older children, the progressive training may not be as necessary as long as a complete verbal description of why he is being punished, how he is being punished, and for how long he is to be punished occurs at the time of the misbehavior and at the time the punishment goes into effect. The child's verbal and memory capabilities will help bridge the time.

In summary, then, it is best to use punishment as soon after the misbehavior as possible. When immediate punishment is impossible, the parent should make sure a complete verbal explanation is given to the child. When possible, the child should be trained to accept progressively longer delays between his misbehavior and the punishment.

How Severe Should the Punishment Be?

If a parent wants punishment to be as effective as possible, the parent would severely punish the child each time the child misbehaved. Using less severe punishment is not likely to be as effective in changing the child's behavior, and the child is more likely to repeat the behavior in the future. When very severe punishment is used, the behavior is generally suppressed completely and does not occur again in the future.

Although the above statements certainly are true, it is best to carefully consider other consequences of using very severe punishment. Severe punishment, although more effective in changing behavior, is also more likely to produce strong emotional reactions in the child. Besides, *it is very important that the consequences be fair,* and it doesn't seem that severe punishment could be fairly applied to all misbehaviors. If the misbehavior has important consequences (such as the case of the child putting a blanket over the baby's face), then it would be reasonable to use a severe form of punishment. If the child's misbehavior is less important (such as spilling food at the table), less severe punishment would be in order. *The fairness rule would suggest that the punishment match the misbehavior: A behavior that has important consequences if continued should be punished more severely than a behavior of lesser importance.*

The fairness rule can be made to be very workable if the parent conscientiously combines punishment with a good amount of positive interaction when the child is behaving appropriately. If punishment alone is used to direct a child's behavior, the parent will be forced to use more severe forms of punishment to control the child's behavior.

How Often Should the Behavior Be Punished?

Punishment, to have the greatest effect on a behavior, should occur every time the inappropriate behavior occurs. When we punish a behavior only occasionally, the behavior will persist for longer periods and be more difficult to stop entirely.

Punishing every occurrence, although the most effective approach, is often impractical, and the consequences of less frequent punishment should be considered. Let's look at two situations where a parent cannot or does not punish every occurrence of the behavior, and at the effects of occasional punishment on the child's behavior. In our first example, the parent does not punish every occurrence of the behavior because some instances of the behavior occur when the parent is not with the child. For example, the child may engage in the behavior when he is at a friend's house or at school. What is the effect of the child not being punished? What will happen is that the child will learn to discriminate the occasions when the behavior is likely to be punished and those where it will not. In other words, he is more likely to misbehave in those situations where he has not been punished than in those situations where he has previously been punished.

In the second case the parent, because of his shifting moods or general lack of consistency, only punishes the child on certain occasions. At other times the behavior goes unpunished, or in some cases the parent may even encourage the behavior by laughing at the child. The laughing or attention might be a powerful reward for the child's behavior. In this situation, what is the parent teaching the child? Probably very little. The parent's inconsistency will only confuse the child and, when he is punished, he will become upset because of the unfairness of treatment. If the child is very alert, he may be able to "read" the parent's mood and discriminate which mood is a signal indicating the behavior is acceptable and which mood is a signal for not doing the behavior. The behavior will then occur only when the parent is in a permissive mood.

Two additional ways of increasing the effectiveness of punishment are (1) telling the child precisely what he is being punished for, and (2) using an overcorrection procedure. *Verbal feedback*—telling the child what he is being punished for—greatly improves the effectiveness of punishment. For example, in an important study psychologists Baron and Kaufman demonstrated that punishment, by itself, was far less effective than punishment combined with instructions concerning what was the appropriate behavior.[1] This makes sense. When a child misbehaves, he might not have been aware that the behavior was inappropriate. He also might not have been aware of what was a more appropriate behavior.

[1]Baron, A. and Kaufman, A. Human Free Operant Avoidance of "Time Out" from Monetary Reinforcement. *Journal of the Experimental Analysis of Behavior,* 1966, Vol. 9, pp. 557-565.

It is best to be quite descriptive rather than general when telling a child why he is being punished. Note the different amount of information in these messages: "I'm sending you to your room because you've been acting silly" compared to "I'm sending you to your room because you were running through the house and talking loudly when I asked you not to. I wanted you to play quietly." In the first message, the child might be unsure of what the parent meant by "acting silly." It could have meant running around, or talking too loud, or some other behavior that the mother was not concerned with. In the second message, there can be no mistake what the mother is punishing the child for. He was running through the house and making noise following a request to not do these things. The parent makes the message even more complete by telling the child what would have been an appropriate—and unpunished—way of behaving.

Overcorrection is a relatively new procedure that psychologists have been using with children to improve the effectiveness of punishment. Azrin, Kaplan, Foxx, three psychologists who have worked extensively with children, have described two types of overcorrection procedures: restitutional overcorrection and positive practice.[2]

Restitutional overcorrection requires a child to correct the effects or consequences of his misbehavior to a better-than-normal state. For example, suppose your child was playing in his room and scribbled on his wall with a crayon. You could spank the child or punish him in some other way, or you could use restitutional overcorrection. If you used restitutional overcorrection, you might have the child wash the wall where he scribbled. In addition, you would have the child *overcorrect* his misbehavior by washing an additional section of the wall. Restitutional overcorrection is similar to using isolation (the child can't be doing something else which is more enjoyable while washing the walls) as well as making the child behave responsibly and correct his actions.

Positive practice overcorrection requires the child to practice correct behaviors whenever an example of the misbehavior occurs. For example, a child who comes home from school and, when he enters the door, drops his coat on the floor. This child might be made to go outside, come in the door, take his coat off and hang it in the closet. The child may be made to positive practice several times following each occasion of the misbehavior.

[2]Azrin, N.H., Kaplan, S.J., and Foxx, R.M. Autism Reversal: Eliminating Self-Stimulation of Retarded Individuals. *American Journal of Mental Deficiency,* 1973, Vol. 78, pp. 241-248.

The logic behind overcorrection procedures, especially positive practice, is that a child who is simply punished is not given practice doing a more appropriate behavior. Overcorrection combines the effectiveness of isolation with practicing appropriate behavior.

In summary, we have seen that punishment can be made more effective if the child is punished immediately after he commits the misbehavior, if the punishment is rather severe, if the punishment occurs every time the child commits the misbehavior, if the child is told explicitly why he is being punished (and what would have been a more appropriate behavior), and if an overcorrection procedure is used in addition to the punishment.

PUNISHMENT: GOOD OR BAD?

When a parent punishes a child, there can be desirable effects: the behavior that was of concern may not occur again, or it may occur less often. These are the desirable effects of punishment and what a parent hopes to achieve when punishing his child. These positive side effects are most likely to occur if punishment has been combined with positive methods for encouraging appropriate behaviors. Sometimes, however, we produce effects that we don't want. One such effect that we've already discussed is that the behavior does not change as we had hoped but may actually occur more often. When this happens, we have not really punished the child in the strict definition of punishment. In fact, what might be happening is the attention the child receives may actually be increasing the child's inappropriate behavior. This does sometimes occur when the child receives little attention from his parents and others. But the most undesirable effect of punishment is the increase in the emotional behaviors of the child. These can occur in several forms: counteraggression, avoidance, and an increase in anxiety. These emotional reactions can be considered as the undesirable by-products or side effects of punishment.

When a child shows these emotional side effects, parents often react inappropriately. The parent sees the child's reactions as being intentional, and the parent reacts by punishing the child again. Unfortunately, the parent is not aware that it was the punishment that produced the emotional side effects and not some conscious choice on the part of the child. When the parent becomes upset when one of the negative side effects occurs and punishes the child again, he is being caught up in a vicious circle: the punishment produces a negative side effect, which causes the parent to punish the child again, which causes another negative side effect. And on and on it goes. If, on the other hand, the parent is aware that negative side effects are natural by-products of punishment, he will be less likely to punish again and will end the vicious circle. Let's look at some of the side effects so you will be able to recognize them for what they are and will be better able to prevent the occurrence of the vicious circle.

Counteraggression

Counteraggression is one of the more common side effects of punishment, especially physical punishment. Counteraggression means that when the child is punished, he will either physically or verbally strike out at the person doing the punishing. Most of us have experienced this. We have caught our child doing something we feel is inappropriate and have quickly spanked the child. The child might react by saying, "I hate you," or he might even hit back. This is a very natural reaction to pain. In fact, many studies have shown that pain is one of the most important causes of aggression. Your child is reflexively reacting to the pain of punishment.

If the child does strike out, what do you usually do? You punish him even more severely. Fortunately, most children learn after several episides of this to control this anger. The child still feels aggressive toward the person who has punished him, but he may not demonstrate it immediately. He may even direct his aggression toward some other, safe object such as a smaller child or a toy.

Avoidance

Avoidance reactions are more subtle and less obvious reactions to punishment. When a child is punished, he is less likely to come near the person who has punished him. This obviously prevents the parent from having more positive interactions with the child.

Avoidance reactions can be of two types. First, the child can physically avoid his parents, or he can psychologically avoid them. A good example of psychological avoidance is a common classroom situation. A child who has been reprimanded or punished by his teacher for wrong answers might begin to avoid his schoolwork. He can't be wrong if he hasn't tried to learn the material. Now if the child is asked a question, rather than saying the wrong answer he will either not answer or say "I don't know." This is often less punishing than being wrong and being told so by his teacher.

Increased Emotionality

A child who has been severely punished will often show increased emotionality or anxiety. Possibly a child should feel some form of guilt or anxiety when he has engaged in an inappropriate behavior, but this is not the type of emotionality I'm primarily concerned with. What is of concern is the emotionality that a child shows when he is afraid to approach and talk to someone because this person has frequently punished the child. This child may also carry his fears and anxiety to other situations. He is afraid to play with others because he fears he will be punished. He is afraid to laugh and enjoy the company of others because of his fear of being punished. This is not an unusual by-product of an extensive use of punishment—particularly when the child has been punished frequently and unfairly.

A child who shows this maladaptive anxiety may have problems in other situations. In school he is timid and afraid because, in the past, if he misbehaved, he was punished. The child's pattern of behavior is one that will prevent him from getting close to people and establishing a warm, positive relationship with someone.

CONCLUSIONS

Punishment can be an effective tool for parents to use to teach their children how to behave appropriately, but punishment because of its effectiveness often becomes the main strategy a parent uses to interact with his child. This leads to the use of punishment when other methods of interaction are not only more appropriate, but would accomplish the teaching job more effectively. A parent should choose punishment as a teaching tool only after thinking of the consequences punishment can have on the child's other behaviors and the relationship between the child and his parents. If punishment seems to be the most effective tool for accomplishing what the parent wants, then it should be used—but used knowledgeably.

EXAMPLE 5.1

Control Over Self-Injurious Behavior

Some children with severe emotional problems begin to injure themselves. Sometimes this self-injurious behavior becomes so bad that the children must be physically restrained to keep them from poking out their eyes, pulling out their hair, or biting themselves and drawing blood. What can be done to eliminate these severe behaviors? Lovaas and Simmons have reported research on this problem. They requested children from two hospitals in California for their study. They wanted children who were the most self-destructive children in the hospitals. The children they received certainly were self-destructive. The three children selected for the study all had to have their hands tied so as to prevent them from beating on themselves. The self-injurious behavior had been going on for years with little relief except when the children were tied up.

The first strategy Lovaas and Simmons tried was to just let the children bang on themselves. Hopefully they would stop—sometime. This worked, but slowly. It took many, many days for the children to stop beating on themselves. Next they decided to punish the children each time they hit themselves. The punishment used was a brief electrical shock to the body. The effects were unbelievable! It took just a few shocks to stop the children from hurting themselves.

This study was excellent in pointing out that sometimes punishment can be very effective for eliminating behaviors. These children, some of whom had been self-injurious for many years, were taught not to hurt themselves in just a few days using the punishment procedure.

Once the children were no longer hitting themselves, Drs. Lovaas and Simmons could then begin teaching them appropriate behaviors. This had been impossible before. Every time the children were freed from their bindings, they began beating on themselves. Punishment eliminated this behavior so they could be taught better ways of behaving.

From I. O. Lovaas and J. Q. Simmons, Manipulation of Self-Destruction in Three Retarded Children. *Journal of Applied Behavior Analysis*, 1969, Vol. 2, pp. 143–157.

EXAMPLE 5.2

Unusual Punishers
Can Work Best—Sometimes

Drs. Madsen and Madsen report an interesting case study which showed how an unusual punisher was effective in changing behavior when a more common one wasn't. The case involved a three-year-old boy who bit his sister three or four times daily. At first the mother tried severely reprimanding the child and slapping him every time he bit his sister. The biting actually increased. The mother tried a new approach. She told her three-year-old son, "When you want to bite, your mouth must be clean. When you want to bite, you may, but your mouth must be clean so your sister doesn't get sick from the dirty germs. When you want to bite, come and tell Mother, and I will make sure your mouth is clean." The boy did come to his mother once, but she had the boy rinse out his own mouth with a liquid dishwashing soap. The biting was eliminated.

This case shows how important it is to be aware of the effects of your behavior on your child. Most mothers would have thought the child was being punished when slapped, but, in fact, the slapping was causing biting to occur more often. When the mother changed her strategy and told the child he could bite if his mouth was clean, the child stopped biting.

From C. K. Madsen and C. H. Madsen, *Parents/Children/Discipline: A Positive Approach*. Boston: Allyn and Bacon, 1970. Example 60.

EXERCISE

I would like you to consider two exercises. The first I would label as an awareness exercise and the second is of more practical value.

Exercise 1: Awareness

What effect does your mood have on your children when you punish them? Your mood can be expressed in a number of ways, such as facial expressions and tone of voice. The effects of these expressions are usually in your child's emotional responses, but can also occur in how well the punishment reduces the behavior. For example, an experiment by Dr. O'Leary and some of his colleagues at the State University of New York, Stony Brook, showed that when teachers reprimanded children in a soft voice, they reduced problem behaviors more then when loud reprimands were used.[3]

What effect does your mood have on your children's behavior? Check this out. Try reprimanding or using other punishers in a quiet, matter-of-fact manner. Notice if this reduces emotional behavior. It should.

Exercise 2: Positive Practice

Choose a behavior that your child engages in that frequently produces reprimands from you. Now, when the child engages in the behavior of concern, make him practice a more appropriate behavior. Have him practice the appropriate behavior five times! For example, if your child doesn't pick up his clothes, have him practice putting his clothes where they belong. Then take the clothes and put them back where they were. Do this five times. Again, it is important to do this in a matter-of-fact manner. You shouldn't show anger, nor should you make a game of it. What you are trying to do is give the child practice engaging in an appropriate behavior. At the same time you are punishing the inappropriate behavior by not letting him play until he has completed his positive practice.

You should find that several episodes of positive practice will virtually eliminate the inappropriate behavior. It may take a few minutes of your time, but the result of having the child engage in a more appropriate behavior and your not having to remind or reprimand as often should make the time spent worthwhile.

---

[3]O'Leary, K.D., Kaufman, K.F., Kass, R.E., and Drabmann, R.S. The Effects of Loud and Soft Reprimands on the Behavior of Disruptive Students. *Exceptional Children,* 1970, Vol. 37, pp. 145-155.

6

Using Rewards
To Create
A Positive
Relationship

Several students in a university class were working on a special project; they were trying to teach retarded children to talk. The retarded
children could all understand some spoken commands, but few could
speak appropriate words and sentences. The results were amazing.
The retarded children after just a few weeks were able to correctly say
many new words. Some were even speaking in short sentences. How
had these children learned? What had the students done to teach the
children to talk? The students had used one of the simplest and yet
most powerful teaching methods available. They rewarded the children
for speaking.

Most psychologists and others working with children agree that
children will learn new behaviors that produce rewards. Often, when
we think of rewards, we think only of things such as money, candy,
and so on. This is only partly correct. People who have studied how
children learn, view rewards quite differently.

WHAT ARE REWARDS?

When you ask a psychologist to give you a definition of a *reward* he generally won't mention things like money or candy (except as examples). What he will tell you is that *rewards are things which follow a particular behavior and increase the likelihood that the behavior will be repeated more frequently in the future.* OK, that sounds good, but what does it mean? It means that a reward is defined in terms of how it affects behavior. It is not something we merely think a child might like. It is something that actually increases a child's future behavior when it follows an instance of that behavior.

Let's look at an example. Consider a mother who brought her six-year-old child home from the hospital where he had spent two months recovering from a severe operation. The child, when he arrived home, spent all his time following his mother around or demanding her time. When the mother tried to get the child to play with his friends, the child refused. After two weeks, the mother was becoming concerned with her child's lack of social behavior. To encourage her child to play with his friends, she invited two of his friends to visit him. At first her child simply sat and watched his friends play a game. After a while one of the child's friends made an incorrect move and the child said, "Here, let me show you how to do that." The mother immediately walked up to the children and said, "It is so nice to see you playing together. Here, I've brought you some Coke and cookies. If you can play nicely for fifteen more minutes, I have a nice surprise for all of you." Within a few minutes, the child was lost in play. The mother was sure that he would be, but the problem was how to get him to play in the first place. Her use of a "surprise" which she knew would excite the child (she had used the promise of a surprise to keep the child's spirits up while he was at the hospital) made use of her knowledge of the child's unique interests to find a reward. It worked! The child played with his friends.

Sound familiar? Of course it does. Most parents use rewards all the time. Maybe they don't call them rewards, but whenever they show approval for their child's behavior, they are rewarding the child. I suppose this is why most parents quickly learn to use rewards to teach their children. They have already used rewards in the past and have seen how important they are for teaching children. But to use rewards most effectively, parents should be aware of how rewards work. The purpose of this chapter is to describe what rewards are and how they can be used most effectively by parents.

The above example points out several important features of rewards: (1) rewards are things that increase future occurrences of a behavior; (2) rewards come after an instance of the desired behavior; and (3) rewards are different things for different people.

What, then, are rewards? Rewards are things children (and other people) receive after they have completed some behavior. The reward will then increase the likelihood that the child will do the behavior again and again.

People sometimes have wrong ideas about what rewards are and what they are intended to do. Many people, although they actually use rewards with their own children, have equated rewards with bribes, which they feel are bad. Is there a difference between a reward and a bribe? I think there is an important difference. When we think of bribes, what do we think of? A criminal telling a judge, "If you let me off with a light sentence, I'll make sure you never have to work another day in your life"? A bribe? Yes. But notice what the criminal is doing: he is paying the judge for undesirable behavior or to avoid the consequences of aversive behavior. Rewards, on the other hand, are consequences for desirable behavior. This difference won't mean much to some people who are opposed to any kind of "payoff"—regardless of whether it is for good or for bad behavior.

I once heard a father, who was also a prominent physician, say, "I refuse to give my child a reward for making his bed [which the child never did and which caused his parents to yell at him], that's just something he should do. It is the right thing. I won't pay him for doing something he is supposed to do." What is the father saying? One thing the father is saying is that doing good things shouldn't have to be rewarded. I asked the physician if he thought his work—helping people who are sick—was a good thing. He said yes. Then should he be paid for his work? He probably would stop helping sick people if he wasn't paid for his work. This might not make us happy to know, but it is a fact of life. People do those things that produce payoffs. Children are no different. They have to receive payment if they are to learn new and appropriate ways of acting.

HOW DO REWARDS WORK?

Rewarding a child for a particular behavior does two things: it increases the likelihood that the behavior will be repeated, and it directs the behavior. That is, rewards not only make the child more willing to do the behavior again, but rewards also make the child aware of which behaviors the parents approve of and wish to encourage.

Let's use a hypothetical example to explain these two functions of rewards. Suppose you were taking a long trip in your car. On the first day of the trip you noticed your children sometimes sat quietly and read books or played with toys. Other times they would fidget and fight with one another. Because the children were so much more pleasant to be with when they were not fidgeting and fighting, you decided to give them a treat when they were being quiet. The effect of the treat was interesting—the children sat quietly for longer periods of time. After a while one of the children began fidgeting and the other child said, "Don't do that, Mom wants us to be quiet."

Our hypothetical example describes the two effects of rewards: they increased the amount of time the children sat quietly, and they gave the children feedback on which behaviors you preferred the children to engage in.

In the example the parent, rather than giving the children a treat, might have told them a story, played a game with them, or several other things. There are many different kinds of rewards parents can use with children.

Types of Rewards

For convenience, let's make some categories of the types of rewards. We can divide possible rewards into five main categories: object rewards, activity rewards, social rewards, personal (self) rewards, and token rewards. Keep in mind that the categories and the examples in each category may or may not be rewarding for a given child. The test to determine if something is really rewarding is if it increases the behavior it follows. Notice that all rewards have several things in common. First, they are things, activities, and so on that the child likes. To tell a child who hates spinach that if he hurries and finishes playing with his toys he can have some spinach is obviously not a very rewarding prospect for the child. A second feature common to rewards is that they are not normally available to the child. For example, if we wanted to use going to a movie as a reward, then the child should not normally be allowed to go to movies any time he wants. Why should a child work to get something he has access to all the time? This, then, implies the third feature of rewards: rewards should only be gained by performing the desired behavior. This does not mean that all of a child's activities should be restricted and only doled out as rewards. Rather, some (but not all) special activities beyond what the child normally receives should be used as rewards. For example, if you give your child a weekly allowance, you might give him additional money as a reward for engaging in certain desired behaviors. Or a parent who normally puts his child to bed at nine might say, "Johnny, if you eat your dinner, you can watch the ten o'clock special on TV tonight."

Object Rewards. Object rewards are things you give a child that he can touch, manipulate, eat, hug, and so on. These are physical things—things that can be played with, eaten, or thrown away.

An object reward, for example, might be candy. A parent might wish to reward his child with candy in the following way.

Parent: (*to her six-year-old girl*) Mary, I think you are old enough to make your bed each morning before you go to school. I'll show you how today and then you try. If you can do a good job, I'll let you take a candy bar in your lunch. I'll help you for a few days until you can do it by yourself. Remember, do a good job and I'll give you a candy bar to take in your lunch.

The actual reward might have been something else, such as a toy, but the idea is that an object reward is something that the child can hold, touch, eat, or play with.

Object rewards have several advantages and disadvantages that should be considered. The major advantage is that the reward is something that makes the child feel good, often for a period of time after the reward has been given. Some object rewards, such as toys, persist for a long period of time and help the parent to set the stage for changing another behavior. A parent might say, for example, "John, do you remember why you got that little truck?" After the child is reminded of his success and the consequences of his behavior, the parent can then describe the behavior that he now wishes to change and the consequences for changing the behavior. The object reward that the child already owns will encourage him to change his behavior so that he might receive the next. A second advantage of object rewards is that they stimulate a number of sense modalities. Notice a child, especially a small child, who is eating a candy bar. He not only eats it, he fondles it, he licks it, he looks at it; in other words, it stimulates a number of his senses. And we can find pleasure through all of our senses.

Object rewards do have disadvantages. The most important disadvantage is the cost of the reward. If we rewarded a child with a candy bar each time he engaged in an appropriate behavior, we might have a well-behaved, plump child who had poverty-stricken parents. A second disadvantage is that object rewards cannot always be given immediately after the child has engaged in the desired behavior. Earlier, we discussed that punishment, to be most effective, should follow the undesirable act closely in time. The same is true for rewards. Rewards that are most effective are those that immediately follow the desired behavior.

Activity Rewards. This class of rewards is one of the potentially most valuable a parent can use. Activity rewards are rewards where a child earns the right to engage in some desired activity. Good examples of activity rewards are going to grandmother's, or staying up late to watch a special television show.

Often these special activities are already available to the child, but the reason he gets to do them is not defined to the child. For example, a parent might say to his spouse, "The kids have been really nice today, let's take them for a ride in the car." A reward? Yes, for most children getting to go for a ride with parents is potentially a powerful reward. But in this case, it was used in a less-than-optimum fashion. The children were not told why they were going for the ride; also, for rewards to be most effective the rules for gaining them should be specified ahead of time. A more efficient use of riding in the car as a reward might have been if the father had told the children when he got home from work, "Mom says that you've been super today. That makes me happy. If you are nice the rest of the day—until after dinner—we'll go for a ride in the car. OK?" Here the possible reward is described to the child, as is the behavior that is necessary to obtain the reward.

A good example of the use of an unusual activity reward was described by Dr. Lloyd Homme and his colleagues who were working with underachievers in a classroom setting. He told the children that if they worked at their materials and remained in their seats for a specified period of time, they could "run and act crazy." They worked like little demons, and they ran and acted crazy when the reward time came.[1] This example is instructive. More than just describing an unusual and fun reward situation, Homme's study showed how one activity can be used to reward another activity. Homme, after using a number of similar activity rewards, formulated a very powerful rule describing the relationship between any two activities the child might engage in. The rule, which Dr. Homme labeled the "Grandmother's rule," stated that any activity that the child frequently engaged in by his own choice could be used as a reward for the child's engaging in any other activity that the child did less frequently. Or, as Grandmother might put it, "You can have some ice cream after you have finished eating your peas."

This rule is a natural for parents. Most of us use it all the time. Think of a recent example when you've told your child something similar. You might have said, "You can go outside and play just as soon as you've finished doing your homework." What you were doing when you did this was to use one of the most powerful teaching devices that has been described by psychologists. The reason that most parents use this rule (whether or not they have thought of it as a rule) is because it works so well and because of its simplicity.

As you look at other examples of using rewards, you'll find that you've probably used all of them on one occasion or another. It doesn't take a psychologist to tell you that they work to teach a child. What the psychologist can tell you, however, is how you might improve the way you are using rewards. For example, let's look at another example of a parent who uses an activity that the child enjoys to reward the child for doing something that is less desirable. The child has brought home some schoolwork, but rather than doing the work he sits down in front of the television. The child's mother asks, "Don't you have some homework to do?" The child says, "Yes, I'll

[1]Homme, L.E., de Baca, P.C., Levine, J.V., Steinhorst, R., and Rickert, E.J. Use of the Premack Principle in Controlling the Behavior of Nursery School Children. *Journal of the Experimental Analysis of Behavior,* 1963, Vol. 6, p. 544.

do it as soon as I finish this TV program." "OK," says the parent, "but make sure you do." Here we have a situation where the child has two activities available to him and one is more desirable than the other. Remembering "Grandmother's rule," we say that we can reward doing schoolwork (a less desirable activity) by using watching television (a more desirable activity) as the reward. Has the parent in this example used "Grandmother's rule"? No! The reason is that for rewards to be effective they must *follow* the behavior that we wish to encourage. In the example, the child should have been told, "You may watch television as soon as you have correctly completed your homework." In the first case, the child probably wouldn't have worked on his homework until the mother got on his back because he already had what he wanted: watching television. In the second case, the child probably would have hurried in to do his homework because the sooner he completed the work, the sooner he could watch television.

Activity rewards have several advantages: they are things that the child likes to do, and they are usually inexpensive. The one difficulty with using activity rewards is that the child's interests change, and what the parent thought might be a rewarding activity might, at that point in time, not be very interesting and therefore not very rewarding for the child. We can get around this problem in two ways. First, rather than telling the child that he can do just one thing after he completed the activity to be rewarded, we can give him several choices. For example, we might tell the child, "When you've finished your homework, you can either watch TV or we can start putting together that model airplane you received for your birthday." Here the child has the choices of two activities, one of which may interest him.

The second way of making sure that a potentially rewarding activity is available to the child is to let the child tell you what he would like to do. In the above example the parent might have said, "When you've finished your homework, you can either watch TV or we can start putting together that model airplane you received for your birthday, *or you can suggest something you would like to do.*" You sometimes have to monitor the child's choices to make sure that he doesn't expect too large a payoff, but after doing this a few times, the child will probably act fairly in choosing his reward.

Social Rewards. These rewards are so commonly used that sometimes we don't think of them as rewards. Social rewards are the people or interaction rewards such as praise, smiles, and pats on the back. These rewards are subtle—and yet so powerful. All we have to do is think of our own feelings when someone whom we respect has paid us a compliment to understand how powerful social rewards can be. I remember, for example, one time when I had attempted to write fiction and a person whom I considered a very good writer said that he thought my story was good. I beamed, and for days afterwards I replayed in my mind what he had said. It was a great feeling. I rushed back to my typewriter and began banging out another story. We've all had similar experiences many times in our lives. The same thing occurs when a child is complimented or in some way told that his behavior meets with approval of someone he respects. The compliment or social reward not only makes him feel good, but it increases the likelihood that the child will behave in similar ways in the future. And aren't these the important effects of rewards—to motivate and to direct behavior?

Most of the social rewards young children receive come from their parents, and if the parent and the children have good relationships, the parent's praise is an extremely powerful reward for the children. After all, probably the people most respected by a young child are his parents. As the child gets older, other people also become important sources of social rewards. For example, when a child enters school, his friends, classmates, and teachers provide him with many social rewards. Later, some of the most important rewards will be controlled by the boy or girl whom the child is dating (or wishes to date). The rewards delivered by these people will greatly influence the child's behavior. For example, a ten-year-old child's choice of clothing, talk away from home, and so on are much more likely to be influenced by the social rewards provided by his peers than by his parents. The effect the rewards from peers and others will have on the child's behavior depends on several things: (1) how consistent the rewarded behaviors are with those his parents reward—if the parents frequently reward certain behaviors, they will be more resistant to change than less frequently rewarded behaviors; (2) the importance of the peers rewards for the child—if the child receives few rewards at home, he is more likely to engage in behaviors that are rewarded by his peers; (3) the behaviors being rewarded—if the behaviors are important to his relationships with his peers, then his peers will possess the most powerful rewards for these behaviors.

Social rewards have the advantage that they can be used lavishly without financial cost to parents. There are so many ways of telling a child that you approve of his behavior. A smile, at times, can communicate a parent's satisfaction; a hug can make a child feel fantastic; and a simple compliment such as "Gee, I sure like the way you share your toys with your little sister" can make a child's day. It is because of the ease with which social reinforcers can be used that I'm surprised that they are not used more often. I remember a case where I was talking to a parent about his child and the parent complained that his child never settled down and acted quiet. While the parent was saying this, his child was sitting and playing quietly. When I asked the parent why he didn't compliment the child on his good behavior (sitting and playing), the parent replied, "I'm not going to bother him; this is the first time all day he has been good. I'm not going to get him going."

If the parent had praised the child's behavior, it is very likely that the child would increase his sitting and playing—a behavior that is certainly more desirable than some of the negative forms of behavior that parents typically complain about.

Social rewards are not the final solution to training children. There are problems with the use of social rewards that a parent must be aware of. First, and probably the most important, is the problem of hypocrisy. Imagine this situation: A parent who is constantly yelling at his spouse tells his child, "Son, it is important to be polite to others." The parent wants to increase his child's polite interactions with the other children in the family. When the child is polite, the parent compliments the child. Is it likely that the parent's praise will increase his child's polite behavior? Maybe. But there is a problem here; the child is getting two sources of information. First, the parent is telling the child that he approves of the child's polite behavior, but the child is also observing his father and mother not being polite to one another. Here we have a situation where the parent says one thing and does another. There is a strong lack of consistency between word and deed, a situation that often leads to a breakdown in the control exerted by social reinforcement. The child may learn to say the same things that his parent says about the importance of being polite, but he is also likely to behave toward others in the same way his parent does. What this comes down to is that if you want social reinforcement to be an effective tool for teaching your child, the social reinforcement you use should be consistent with your own behavior. If it isn't, and if what you are trying to teach your child is important to you, then it is important for you to change your behavior to be consistent with what you are trying to teach your child.

A second problem with social rewards is that they will not continue to be effective if they are used without occasionally being associated with something more tangible, such as an object or an activity reward. For example, if you are trying to increase the amount of time your child plays with other children without fighting, you should occasionally do something like this:

Parent: Johnny, it's so nice to see you and your friends playing together with your cars. Since you are being such good boys, I'm going to give you a popsicle.

Most of the time the parent could just compliment the child, but occasionally it is important to remind the child that when you are happy with his behavior, you are more likely to do nice things for him. This is the way most parents interact with their children. When they are mad, they are less likely to do nice things for their children, but when happy and pleased with the child, they play with him, share things with him, and give him things. This should be communicated to the child. He shouldn't feel that "it doesn't matter if Mom and Dad say I'm nice or not, they still don't play with me or give me things."

Try using a lot of praise with your children. You'll find that not only will their behavior change, but you will feel better about your relationship with your children. Al Capp's Mammy Yokum says it nicely: "It's better to be good because it's nicer."

Personal Rewards.   These are not rewards that you give the child, but rewards he gives himself. Watch a child playing sometime and notice what he does when he accomplishes the goal of his play. If the child is a toddler, he will clap his hands, smile, or in some other way show pleasure. If the child is older, he may say to himself, "Gee, that's neat," or something equivalent. What the children are doing is giving themselves a reward. We all do this. Call it pride, happiness with a job well done, pleasure with our work, or whatever, the end result is that we are rewarding ourselves.

If you were to analyze your self-rewarding, you might think that it is just natural to self-reward, but is it? This has been the subject of a number of research studies, and the results have generally shown that children tend to evaluate (self-reward) their behavior in much the same way that the child's parents have evaluated the behavior. If a parent expects a great deal from the child, the child will only self-reward when he has accomplished what he thinks the parent expects of him. A child whose parent expects less will reward himself for less output.

When children are berated by their parents and seem to never be able to do anything that meets with their parents' approval, they will have the same feelings about themselves. They criticize their performance and put themselves down. They act in such ways that we might label them as having an inferiority complex." They feel they are not as good as others.

Personal rewards, therefore, are the product of learning. The child learns to evaluate his behavior, and the framework of evaluation is that which he has been taught. If you see a child who evaluates his own behavior as inadequate when other sources of information indicate that the child has performed adequately, then we can expect to find that the child has someone in his environment who has taught the child how to negatively evaluate his behavior.

Another way that rewards affect a child's negative self-evaluation is when he finds that negative evaluations produce parental attention. Let's look at how this might occur. Mark, a normal little boy, has parents who are aloof and rather cold in their interpersonal activities with others. Their reactions to their child's performance is matter of fact and on the cool side. They desire that Mark become successful in life and direct him toward activities they feel will insure his success. Mark receives little attention from his parents except that which is directed toward bettering himself in gentlemanly ways. Mark found that if he acted unhappy or discouraged with his performance, his parents would immediately rush to insure Mark that he was doing a good job. They would also spend time talking to him to help him "work through his problem." This was about the only time the parents paid attention to him that wasn't directed toward his learning to read, play the piano, and so on. Mark was being taught that if he wanted his parents' attention, he could get it by being a failure or acting as if he was unhappy because of his personally evaluated inadequacy. But beyond his interactions with his parents, Mark was also using this successful attention-getting strategy with other people. Others, by reacting in a compassionate way when Mark acted inadequate, were actually increasing Mark's personal evaluations of inadequacy.

We have seen two different ways in which a child can learn to evaluate his behavior as inadequate. Both of these children would be considered by others as having a poor self-concept—which they have.

We can reverse a child's feelings of inadequacy or, for that matter, teach a child to be more positive in his self-evaluations (self-rewards) by frequently rewarding his achievements. This is not to say that a child should be praised for performances that are lower than what he is capable of, but rewards should be arranged to occur often enough that the child is taught that others evaluate him as being an OK person and one who is capable of doing things that please others. The child who receives this kind of feedback from his parents and others who are important to him will also be learning how to reward his own behavior.

I'm fascinated when I watch a child we might say has self-confidence and a good self-concept. He is willing to try new things, he is capable of making reasonable estimates of his ability to do things, and he doesn't collapse when he occasionally fails at some task. I've observed that parents of such children, in addition to using frequent positive rewards when the child performs adequately, encourage their children to evaluate their behavior in the presence of the parent. For example, a parent might say, "Well that's an interesting picture you've painted. Do you like it?" By doing this the parent is helping the child match his feelings against those of his parents. The child might answer, "Yeah, I think it's neat." And the parent could confirm or change the child's evaluation by saying something like "Yes, I like it, too, but I think the one of the dog is better. Look, you've stayed in the lines with your crayons much better here." The parent accepts the child's feelings and gives him more information for later self-evaluations.

Token Rewards.   If you have ever made a "Good Behavior Chart" for your child and told him that if he does certain things, such as make his bed every day for a week, you will give him a star on his chart and at the end of the week buy him a surprise, you have used token rewards. Token rewards are things that can be used to obtain something else. A token reward can be anything that can be traded for something else. Our economy is set up on a token reward concept. People work and are paid with money, which by itself has no real value. The value of money is what it can be exchanged for. We exchange our money for food (object rewards), to go on vacations (activity rewards), and to buy new clothing (often so that others will admire the way we look and will compliment us on our looks—social rewards). The same type of economy can be used in the home with our children. We give them token rewards which they can later trade for something that is important to them.

Many parents, who feel that their children have responsibilities to help with the everyday activities in the home, like to use a token system rather than giving the child an allowance. The child is given certain duties such as taking out the trash, making his bed before he leaves for school, and keeping the things in his room picked up. Each day the parent inspects the child's room and the garbage container and, if the child has completed his duties, he receives checkmarks on a chart. At the end of the week the child is given the agreed payoff for completing his work. If he has failed to do his duties each day, he is paid less. Sometimes the parent and the child might work out extra duties so that the child can earn extra checkmarks (and therefore, more money) by doing extra jobs around the house. There are several advantages to this system over the allowance system. First, the child is taught that he is responsible for doing things around the house; secondly, the rules which govern how much he will receive are decided before he does the jobs; third, the child learns that he is in control of his earnings—he can earn the money or not, depending on whether or not he does his chores; and fourth, the token program can be used rather than negative methods for governing the child's help in the home.

Token programs work well with children of different ages and, within a family, can be adjusted to each child's age and capabilities. Two parents whom I had the opportunity to work with complained that their children were noncompliant. That is, the children would not do what they were asked to do. When this occurred, the parents usually resorted to yelling at their children. These parents, after deciding what they expected of their three children who ranged in age from two-and-a-half to eleven, told the children they could earn points if they did certain things. The activities requested of each child differed, of course, but each child was expected to do things he was capable of doing. Most of the requests made of the children were associated with complying to the parent's requests. For example, Danielle, a three-year-old girl, was given points whenever she was asked to do a behavior and she promptly did it without saying "I can't" or an equivalent statement. In addition to telling the children what they were expected to do, the parents and children made a "menu" of rewards they could exchange their earned points for. Some of the rewards were inexpensive and could be purchased with little effort on the child's part. Other rewards cost many points and required the child to save his points for several days before he was able to get it. The effect was very good. The children began obeying their parents, the parents only infrequently yelled at their children, and the parents reported that the effect was to make a closer, happier family. I talked to the parents about three months after they had begun the token program and they said they had discontinued using the program. They felt they had improved on their ability to be positive and rewarding, and the children were no longer noncompliant. They did say, however, that the children occasionally asked to have the token program reinstated, but they were usually able to negotiate informal contacts instead. It's possible that the children, when they were asking for the reinstatement, might have been telling their parents that they were not being as rewarding as they were when the program was in operation—a good caution to the parents that they might be slipping.

A good token program such as the one described above has several important features. They are:

1. A token program spells out exactly what is expected of the child.
2. A token program spells out what the parents will do if the child fulfills his part of the agreement.
3. The payoff in the program is fair. That is, it is neither too little payoff nor too much.
4. All parties in the agreement keep their word and fulfill their responsibilities. Guess who generally doesn't fulfill his part of the contract? The child? The parent? You were right if you said the parent. We parents can sometimes get into the habit of saying, "I'll do it later" or "I don't have time right now, maybe tomorrow."

Try using a token program and see what happens. Don't try to work with all of your child's behaviors the first time you use a token program—try one at a time. Select something that you might really wish the child would do more often. A good thing to start on would be something like having the child clean his own room. Sit down with the child and decide what he should do and the payoff for doing it. Make the task expected of the child as specific as possible. For example, you might say he is to have all his toys put in the toy box, his clothing put away, and his shoes in the closet before his bedtime. Also, spell out exactly what the child will receive for his efforts. You'll be pleasantly surprised at how quick and effective the program will be.

EXAMPLE 6.1

Rewards: Are They Bribes?
A Child's View

Do children feel that rewards are bribes? Some do, and this can annoy the child. If a child is annoyed by feelings of being bribed, a frank discussion of what you are trying to accomplish can often help the child understand why you are using rewards. Claire Korn reported this conversation between a counselor and a girl that nicely illustrates why some children might be upset by "bribes."

Counselor (Co): How have things been going at home? Have there been any more fights between your mom and you?

Girl: She's trying to bribe me! She's really trying to bribe me!

Co: What do you mean? What happened?

Girl: She said she would get me a horse if I'd keep my room clean. And that's bribery. Don't you think it's bribery?

Co: Well, it depends on how you look at it. That room is pretty important to your mom and I guess it's so important that she thinks it would be worth even a horse for your room to be kept clean.

Girl: But I do keep it clean. There's nothing on the floor anymore. Of course the bed's not made. But she is trying to bribe me.

Co: What your mother thinks of as being clean isn't the same thing as what you think of as being clean. Do you think it's fair to get something you want for doing something well?

Girl: Yes. But it depends on how you do it. If I got a house or room of my own or something for keeping my room clean, or got a horse for taking care of a dog or something like that— but those aren't good examples—that would be fair.

Co: The reward should somehow be related to—connected to—the thing you being rewarded for?

Girl: Yes, that's it. A horse doesn't have anything to do with a room.

Co: Maybe your mom meant to tie them together somehow, like with responsibility. If you were responsible enough to take care of a horse.

Girl: She did say something about that. But I wouldn't want to take care of the horse anyway. It would have to be boarded.

Why did the girl think she was being bribed? Wasn't it because she wasn't particularly interested in what was being offered as a reward? If the reward offered had been something the girl desired, there probably would not have been the concern about the bribe. But because the horse wasn't desirable, the girl saw her mother's behavior as being bad. We hardly ever see rewards that we think are appropriate as being bribes. Neither do children. To avoid the problem of having a child think of the offered reward as being a bribe, a parent should try to talk with the child and find out what the child would consider an appropriate reward for the desired behavior. You could be surprised what children will say.

From Claire V. Korn, Refusing Reinforcement. In J. D. Krumbholtz and C. E. Thoresen (Eds.), *Behavioral Counseling*. New York: Holt, Rinehart and Winston, 1969. Pp. 45–48.

EXAMPLE 6.2

An Indirect Approach to Changing Behavior

Many of the behaviors a parent wishes to teach a child are difficult to gain direct access to. For example, a parent might wish to reduce the number of times her child "sluffs" school. This can be a difficult problem. The child leaves for school early in the morning, but goes off with his friends rather than going to school. The mother might hear about this only after a week or two. How can the mother change the child's behavior? One way might be to use an indirect approach. Rather than working directly on the sluffing behavior, the parent might choose to work on sluffing by changing another behavior that is incompatible with sluffing. In this case, for example, the mother might wish to reward the child for improving his homework. She could set up a very special reward for the child if he gets his homework correctly done each night. This could be verified by having the teacher send home a note each day that the child turned in his homework. If the child has good incentives for doing his schoolwork, he will be less likely to sluff school. Notice that rewarding the child for doing his schoolwork is much more positive than punishing the child for sluffing. Punishing sluffing might reduce the number of days the child misses school, but will do little to strengthen his doing appropriate schoolwork.

A very dramatic example of how indirect methods can be used to change behavior was described by Dr. Ted Ayllon. One of his patients in a mental hospital wore excessive amounts of clothing, including several sweaters, shawls, dresses, undergarments, and stockings. In addition, she would wrap sheets and towels around her body. Rather than trying to directly teach the woman not to wear the clothing, Ayllon instructed the woman that she was overweight and could not be admitted into the dining area until she lost weight. The easiest way for the woman to lose weight was to remove her excessive clothing. She did—at an average of about two pounds a day, until she—

had shed more than twenty pounds of excess amount of clothing. The program had worked! Rather than working directly on a difficult problem, Dr. Ayllon had handled the problem quickly and efficiently by working on the target behavior by an indirect method.

From T. E. Ayllon, Intensive Treatment of Psychotic Behavior by Stimulus Satiation and Food Reinforcement. *Behavior Research and Therapy,* 1963, Vol. 1, pp. 53–61.

EXAMPLE 6.3

Using Rewards
to Teach a "Vegetative Idiot"

To demonstrate the power of rewards for teaching, Dr. Paul Fuller tried to teach a simple behavior to an eighteen-year-old "vegetative idiot." The boy was so severely retarded that he lay on his back all day. He could not roll over, he was not seen to move his trunk and legs, nor did he make any sounds. His only "behaviors" were slight movement of head and arms. He could also blink and open his mouth. The child, in other words, was nearly a vegetable.

The teaching technique that Fuller used was to squirt a warm sugar-milk solution into the boy's mouth each time the boy moved his arm in an upward direction. Fuller kept increasing the height the boy lifted his arm and after many rewards the arm was moving to a vertical position.

Although the behavior taught to the boy was of no "real value" to the child, it did demonstrate the power of rewards. If rewards could be used to teach a child of such limited capabilities, they should be so much more effective with children of greater capabilities. This has been shown to be true. The use of rewards has been proven to be a very valuable and powerful method for teaching children.

From P. R. Fuller, Operant Conditioning of a Vegetative Human Organism. *American Journal of Psychology,* 1949, Vol. 62, pp. 587–590.

EXERCISE

It is sometimes a good idea to practice something you've read about yourself before actually using it with others. Even though you probably frequently use rewards with your children, you might want to use them more systematically. If so, before you begin a reward program with your children, use one with yourself. This will give you practice using rewards, and you might learn ways of preventing problems when you use a reward program with your children.

A good self-reward program to practice with would be to select some behavior of your own that you would like to change. For example, you may wish to be more friendly with your spouse, to stop chewing your fingernails, or to lose weight. When selecting a behavior to change try to be very specific when defining the behavior. For example, rather than saying, "I want to be a friendlier person," say, "I want to compliment people more often and smile at others more often." The more specific you are, the easier it is to develop a good program. Also, start with something small. Remember, you are practicing. If you try to change many behaviors or a difficult behavior your first time, you may have trouble.

Once you have selected your "target" behavior, make a chart to record your progress. Place the chart in a conspicuous place and tell your family what you are doing. Letting others know what we're doing helps us keep at our task. Then, each time the relevant behavior occurs, mark it on the chart. You'll find that increases in the desirable behavior are very rewarding! But don't rely just on these personal satisfaction rewards. Choose something you want as a reward that you will give to yourself when you achieve your target. Make sure this additional reward is fair and reasonable, however. It doesn't make sense to say, "I'll give myself a manicure if I lose fifty pounds." Nor does it make sense—for most of us—to say, "I'll buy myself a new car if I smile at my spouse five times tomorrow."

If you make a contract with yourself that is fair and reasonable, you should not only see an improvement in your behavior, but you should also learn something about using rewards. I expect you'll see how important a chart is for evaluating your progress, how important immediate rewards are, and how helpful it is to have others help you change your behavior. Good luck!

7

Using Rewards Effectively

When parents use rewards consistently with their children, they will find that the child's behavior will improve, and as an added benefit there is usually a better relationship between parents and children. This happens for several reasons. First, when parents use rewards, there is far less need for the more negative forms of discipline. This was brilliantly shown in a study by Ted Ayllon and M. D. Roberts who were working with children who were very disruptive in a classroom. There were several possible ways they could have decreased the children's disruptive behaviors. They could have punished the children each time they misbehaved, or they could have rewarded them for their good behavior. In the first case the punishment would have decreased the disruptive behavior, but it is unlikely that the children would have learned better ways of behaving in the classroom. Besides, they couldn't be sure that the punishment wouldn't produce undesirable behaviors as a by-product of the punishment. Rewarding good behavior would not only teach the children better ways of behaving, but because the rewards would increase the amount of time the children were behaving appropriately, the amount of disruptive behavior would naturally decrease. This is exactly what happened when Ayllon had the teacher reward the children for appropriate classroom behavior. The children began doing more schoolwork, were far less disruptive, and seemed happier to be in school.[1] This example points out an important rule for social relationships: *good behavior produces positive behavior from others, and negative behavior produces negative behavior from others.*

When we are trying to teach a child a new behavior, whether it is picking up his own clothes or being friendly to his little brother, we can look at the learning process as having two phases. The first phase is when the child is first acquiring the behavior. Here he must start doing things differently than he has in the past. This is a transition between the way he is currently acting and the way we would like him to be acting. The second phase starts after he has learned the new behavior. How can we keep him from forgetting what he has learned and from returning to his other, less desirable way of acting? The two phases require different ways of rewarding the child. In the first phase we are interested in teaching the child as quickly as possible. In the second phase we are interested in making sure the behavior is retained and will not change over time to less desirable forms. Let's look at what is required in each phase.

TEACHING NEW BEHAVIOR

What must be done to teach a child a new behavior? The first thing that should be done is to carefully decide what it is you want to teach. This sounds simple, but it can be an important source of failure for many people who haven't thought it through. Let's look at two examples where parents want to teach their young child to dress himself. The first parent says, "What I want Johnny to do is to learn to dress himself." The second parent says, "I want Johnny to learn to put on his clothing with his shirt, pants, and socks turned right side out and with the front and back properly in place. I also want Johnny to put his shoes on the right feet and lace his own shoes." The first parent

---

[1]Ayllon, T. and Roberts, M.D. Eliminating Discipline Problems by Strengthening Academic Performance. *Journal of Applied Behavior Analysis,* 1974, Vol. 7, pp. 71–76.

might know what he wants, but he has described the behavior too loosely. What exactly does he want his child to do? Will he accept as correct a shirt that is on backward? Shoes that are on the wrong feet? Probably not. When the person doing the teaching has a clear idea of what exactly is to be taught, he can design a better teaching program. We can call this the *goal behavior*—that which we want the child to be able to do when we have taught him. When we have carefully specified the goal behavior, we are in a better position to decide just how we will teach the child.

Let's consider four statements of behaviors that are to be taught. Two of the four will be stated in generalities and are probably inadequate as descriptions of goal behaviors. The other two will be more properly defined. When you have decided which of the two are vague, try to reword them so that they are more specific and descriptive of what the child is to eventually do.

1. I want to teach Johnny to be polite. I want him to respect the rights of others and to be courteous when he is around adults.

2. I want to teach Johnny not to interrupt me when I am on the telephone. I would like to teach him that if he needs me while I am talking on the phone to come to me and tap me on the shoulder rather than yelling at me.

3. I want to teach Johnny to say "er" at the end of words such as *father, other,* and *stutter,* rather than "ah," as he does now.

4. I want to teach Johnny to say his words properly.

Which are the better descriptions of the goal behaviors? The correct answer is numbers 2 and 3. The first description looks pretty good because it describes when the behaviors of being polite should occur, but the definition of what being polite means is left out. Does being polite mean being quiet? Not interrupting others when they are talking? Saying "please" and "thank you" when it is appropriate? Words like *polite* and *courteous* can mean different things to different people. To correctly define what we might desire of Johnny in the first statement we would want to describe exactly what we want him to do in different situations. For example, we might rephrase the definition to include: *I want Johnny to learn to say "thank you" when someone gives him a present or when he has requested something from someone.* It also helps when defining goal behaviors to make up examples for specific situations.

The problem with description number 4 is similar to the first. The statement does not specify clearly what is expected of Johnny. Compare the last statement with the third. The third statement states precisely what Johnny is to learn: to properly use the "er" ending of words. The fourth leaves undefined what it is about saying words that Johnny is to learn.

The reason it is important to specify exactly what you want to teach your child is because it is then much easier to develop a consistent teaching program. Once you have decided upon the goal behavior, you should say, "What is my child doing now?" This is the initial behavior or the behavior you begin working with. The teaching problem is how to get from the initial behavior to the goal behavior as quickly and as enjoyably as possible.

If there is a large difference between what the child is doing now (initial behavior) and the behavior you wish to teach him (goal behavior), you will have to consider how to help the child make the transition to the new behavior. There are basically three ways we can help the child make the transition: shaping, instructions, and modeling (showing). These methods can, and often should, be combined for greatest effectiveness. But for purposes of description let's look at each separately.

Shaping

When a child is first learning a behavior, we can assume either that he is capable of doing the behavior and all that is needed is adequate motivation, or we can assume that the child does not possess the necessary prerequisite behaviors and must be taught these as well as being motivated to learn.

We can assume the child has the necessary prerequisites when the child has, at some time, either successfully performed the behavior that we are wanting to teach or that he has performed other, very similar behaviors. If the child has the prerequisites, our task then is to teach the child to do the behaviors more frequently, in proper sequence or in new situations. This is generally a simpler task than teaching a new behavior to a child who has not acquired the basic skills necessary for the behavior. An example of teaching a child to perform a behavior that he already is capable of, but not performing, is when a child is being taught to ride a bicycle after having previously learned to ride the bicycle with training wheels. If the child has mastered riding the bicycle with training wheels, he has mastered many of the necessary components for riding without the aid of the training wheels. He has, for example, learned to guide the bicycle, to press the pedals in proper sequence, and to apply the brake to stop. What he must now learn is to balance the bicycle and to coordinate the previously learned behaviors while balancing. This is quite a different task than when the child has never acquired these prerequisite components.

To teach a child to engage in a behavior when he has never done it before and has not had much experience with the prerequisite components, we can use a process of teaching which professionals call "shaping." When we shape a child's behavior, we break the complex pattern of behavior down into its component parts and reward the child for successively improving his behavior or for increasing the number of components learned. A friend of mine, for example, tried to teach a retarded girl to walk by herself. The girl initially could stand by holding on to things, and when standing make a few shuffling movements that would transport her over very small distances. My friend felt that this initial behavior was adequate to be shaped into complete and independent walking. His problem was how to teach the girl to make the transition from standing while holding on to furniture and shuffling (initial behavior) to independent walking (goal behavior).

He solved the problem by breaking the goal behavior down into its component parts. To walk, the girl must be able to stand without holding onto something, and she must be able to move her feet in the correct manner without holding onto things.

He started the walking program by holding the girl's hands while she was standing. If she stood while holding his hands, he would smile at her and give her a small taste of ice cream. Once she mastered holding his hands and standing for brief periods, he began rewarding her for standing for longer and longer periods of time. When she was able to stand and hold his hands for two minutes, he started to reduce the support offered with his hands. At first, he would let her hold firmly onto his hands, then only on his fingers, then only on one finger of each hand. This continued until he had her standing without support. Of course, he continued to reward her for any little improvement. Finally, after the girl could stand without support, he would hold the spoon of ice cream a few inches in front of her mouth. To get the ice cream, at first she would only have to lean forward. Later, she had to move one foot forward and so on until she was making several steps to get the ice cream. He had taught her how to walk!

The above is an example of the use of shaping. The trainer broke the behavior down into its basic components, rewarded the girl for each improvement within a component, and when she had mastered one component he rewarded the girl for not only doing the behaviors in that component, but for improving her behavior in the second.

Instructions

Many of the things that are achieved with shaping can be accomplished more easily simply by telling the child what to do. This assumes, of course, that the child has the necessary language skills to understand your words and to follow instructions. When the child has adequate language skills these can be used to simplify the training process, but many of the same rules for shaping apply to the use of instructions to train behavior: the behavior should be broken down into chunks the child is capable of managing, the instructions should be explicit, and the child should be rewarded for each improvement.

Let's look at how the person might train a child to "go to the potty" using shaping procedures and how it can be done much more easily when the child has language skills so that instructions can be used.

To train a child to use the potty using shaping procedures we would reward the child for going into the toilet area, for putting his hands on his pants, pulling his pants down, sitting on the potty, eliminating, and so on. This is a very time-consuming procedure, as those who have trained a preverbal child to use a potty can attest.

If the child had necessary verbal skills, the trainer could have said, "Go into the bathroom." This would replace the several steps of rewarding the child for approaching closer and closer to the bathroom. The same is true with telling the child, "Take down your pants." This replaces several shaping steps of having the child touch his pants, pulling them down a little, and finally pulling them down all the way.

Instructions, then, can be a great shortcut in training the child. But during the initial stages of learning, the child's behavior will occur more rapidly if each appropriate response to the instructions is followed by a reward.

Modeling

Some people who have done research on how children learn have suggested that most of a child's behavior is acquired by watching other people do the behavior and then imitating the model. Because of the importance of imitation learning for children, I will devote two later chapters (9 and 10) to describing modeling and imitative behavior. But because of the similarities between the use of instructions and the use of models for teaching children, a brief description of modeling will be given at this point in the book.

When a parent models a behavior for a child he shows the child what is expected. The showing is done by the parent engaging in the precise activities that he expects the child to do. As with shaping and instructions, modeling is most effective when the behaviors modeled are broken down into small units and the child practices each step before the complexity of the behavior is increased. Again, rewards should follow each improvement.

We have reviewed several procedures for helping a child make the transition from his current behavior (initial behavior) to some goal behavior that we desire. This is learning, but learning where the parent carefully arranges the teaching program so that the child is likely to acquire the behavior in a minimum amount of time and with a minimum of problems. During this phase of learning, the parent should reward the child for each improvement and each time the desired behavior occurs. When a child is learning a new behavior it is important that he receive a great amount of feedback. Rewards provide the feedback and, additionally, motivate the child to continue to learn.

During the initial learning phase, the care taken in the teaching program is critical. For best results, the child should experience as little failure as possible. Failure occurs when the steps being taught are too large or too difficult. If you are unsure of how small to make the steps, make them smaller than you think necessary. If you can see that the child is capable of larger steps, then increase them. If the steps are too large at the beginning, the child will not be able to correctly perform the desired behavior and will not receive the reward. Without rewards he will be less motivated and the feedback on his performance will be less, a situation that can create frustration for both the child and the parent who is trying to teach the child.

MAINTAINING BEHAVIOR THAT HAS BEEN LEARNED

When a child has demonstrated that he understands what the parent wants of him and performs the behavior appropriately, the parent's role changes from teaching the child how to do the behavior to how to maintain the behavior. It is at this point where the question of reinforcing the behavior for each occurrence becomes important. What happens if, after we have taught the child to do some behavior and we have rewarded him for every occurrence of the behavior, the child now finds himself in a situation where he is not being rewarded? Will the child persist with the behavior because he knows it is the right thing to do? Or will the child become frustrated and stop doing the behavior? Research has shown that children who have been rewarded for every occasion of their behavior will rapidly discontinue the behavior if rewards are no longer forthcoming. Often when children discontinue their new behavior they will resort to previous behaviors. This certainly isn't desirable for a parent who has spent time teaching his child a new and better way of behaving.

What can be done to make sure the child retains his newly learned behavior for longer periods of time? It is very unlikely that the child will go through life and be continuously rewarded for his behavior. The answer is to use rewards in a way so as to increase the permanence of the behavior. Remember when I was describing the shaping procedure? When I described how my friend had taught the retarded girl how to walk, I mentioned that at first he rewarded her for standing without holding on for longer and longer periods of time. This is essentially the way we train children to do more and more of the behavior for a reward. Let's use an example to illustrate how we can train children not to rely on rewards for every occurrence of the behavior. Suppose we have successfully taught a child to use the potty, using candies as rewards, but now every time the child goes to the potty, she asks for a candy. What could we do? The first thing we do to systematically withdraw rewards from the training program is to continue to socially reward the child, but withhold candies for every trip to the potty. We might say to the child, "You are a big girl. You don't need candy every time you use the potty. I'll give you a candy next time.'' At first, we might reward her for every other trip to the potty with candy, then for every third time. We would continue over a period of a week or so to reduce the frequency of rewards until we were no longer giving candy for going to the potty. We would continue to praise the child for her successes, however. If we progressively reward fewer and fewer occasions of the behavior, we will find that the child will continue to do the behavior even without the reward. If, on the other hand, we were to discontinue all rewards at once, the child might discontinue doing the behavior altogether.

There is kind of an art to knowing if we are withdrawing rewards too quickly, but we can use the child's behavior as an indication. If the child begins to show signs that the behavior is no longer as accurate or as quick or as well done as before, this is a good sign that we are removing rewards too quickly. If this happens, we should begin to reward the child more frequently and later begin rewarding less often, but reduce our withdrawal program to a slower pace.

Many behaviors that we teach our child persist because they produce natural consequences. For example, the girl that my friend taught to walk did not need to be rewarded with ice cream after a while. Being able to walk around and get things was reward enough. These things that are naturally produced by the behavior are called *natural rewards* and are adequate to support many behaviors. There are some behaviors that are not maintained as easily by natural rewards, and we must continue to reward these behaviors at least occasionally. Behaviors that fit this category are such things as a child's keeping his room picked up. For many children a clean room is just not that important.

We can discover which behaviors should receive occasional rewards by observing the child. Does the child seem to enjoy doing the behavior he has been taught, or does he do it less often than we would hope if we don't encourage (reward) him occasionally? If the child needs occasional encouragement, then we should be careful to use at least occasional social rewards for the child's successful completion of the behavior.

In summary, we have seen that when the child is first learning the behavior he should be rewarded for every occasion of the behavior. Sometimes, in fact, we have to break the behavior down into its components and reward the child for successful completion of just the component. But after the child has mastered the behavior, we want to reward the child less often. We do this not only because it is inconvenient to reward the child every time he does the behavior, but also because less frequent rewards will insure that the behavior will persist longer without being rewarded. When we begin rewarding less often we don't cut out rewards all at once, but we progressively decrease the number of times we reward the child. If his behavior is maintained, we know we have not discontinued rewards too quickly. If the child does not do the behavior as readily, we have discontinued rewards too quickly.

INTENTIONALLY NOT REWARDING

We have seen that rewards can be used to teach children new behaviors. Rewarding children works whether we intentionally reward the child or if the rewards the child receives are delivered unintentionally. Sometimes the unintentional rewards are responsible for many of our children's undesirable behaviors. Many of us have, for example, unintentionally rewarded our child for being loud and obnoxious. Suppose you were talking on the telephone and your child came in and asked for a cookie. Because you were busy, you ignored the child's polite request for a cookie. The child may have thought your ignoring him meant that you had not heard his request so he again asks for a cookie, this time louder than before. Now, you not only heard him, but you are angry that he is talking in such a loud voice and you again refuse to acknowledge his request. The child gets mad and throws a tantrum and yells that he wants a cookie. You become embarrassed because you don't want your friend on the phone to hear your child screaming, so you motion the child to take a cookie. What have you done? You have unintentionally rewarded your child for making loud and demanding requests. This undesirable behavior was rewarded with a cookie where other, more polite requests were ignored.

This type of situation can happen time and time again in the home. The parent refuses to give in to the child's requests until they become obnoxious; then the parent, out of frustration, gives in.

Now that the parent has rewarded the child for this undesirable behavior, how can he undo the damage? We use the reverse of rewarding; we withhold rewards for the undesirable behavior. Withholding rewards for undesirable behavior is technically called *extinction*, and what we are doing when we withhold the rewards is *extinguishing* the child's inappropriate behavior. Let's look at an example of how this works. Dr. Williams provides us with an interesting case. A man and his wife had just brought their child home from the hospital and at night the child would get "upset" for no apparent reason and the parents would go in and comfort the child. After a short period of time the child, whenever he was put to bed, would throw a tantrum and the parents would wait it out for a while and then finally give up and go in to the child. It got to a point where the child wasn't sleeping and the parents were becoming irritable. They decided to solve the problem by just letting the child "cry it out" when he was put to bed. They kept a record of how long the tantrums lasted. The first night the child kicked and screamed for over an hour. The second night the screaming began again but lasted for less time. Within two weeks, the child, when put to bed, would go to sleep without the least bit of crying. This blissful state continued until a babysitter responded to child's slight whimpers. It started the tantrums all over again and the parents had to repeat the whole program again.[2]

Let's review what happened. The parents were naturally concerned with their child's welfare when they brought him home from the hospital, and so whenever the child would cry in bed the parents would check on him. Natural enough—but they were inadvertently rewarding the child for crying. When the child cried the parents would get him up and play with him until he fell asleep. Later, however, there was no longer a need to be concerned with the child's health and the parents no longer responded to the child's weak whimperings and the volume and intensity of the child's tantrums increased until the parents went into his room—rewarding the child for more intense crying. Finally, the parents quit attending to his tantrums and they stopped. Not attending to the tantrums was actually removing the rewards for tantrum behavior. Unfortunately, the babysitter once again rewarded the child for crying and started the whole process over again.

Using extinction can be a very trying experience for two reasons. First, sometimes it seems to take forever for the behavior to decrease. When we first use extinction we can expect the child's inappropriate behavior to actually increase (the child has previously learned to increase the bad behavior to get what he wants) and the behaviors seem to go in a direction opposite of what we want. This is a difficult period

[2]Williams, C.D. The Elimination of Tantrum Behavior by Extinction Methods. *Journal of Abnormal and Social Psychology,* 1959, Vol. 59, p. 269.

for parents, but if they persist in not giving in to the child the behavior will eventually decrease.

If, rather than ignoring the child, the parent gives in to the child's excessive behavior, this excessive behavior will be strengthened and the situation will be worse than when the parent began. Also, if a parent ignores or tries to extinguish a behavior, he should be consistent. If the parent sometimes ignores the behavior but sometimes gives into the child, he may be making the behavior even more difficult to change later on. In the section on maintaining behavior I suggested that behavior, once learned, will persist and be more resistant to extinction if it is only occasionally rewarded. The same is true for inappropriate behavior. If we ignore sometimes and give in sometimes when the child behaves inappropriately, we are making the behavior more resistant to extinction.

The second reason using extinction can be difficult is that we sometimes remove the wrong rewards. Take, for example, a classroom situation where a child has been misbehaving and the teacher has been paying attention to the child's misbehavior. She decides that it is her attention that is maintaining the disruptive behavior and no longer pays attention to the child when he misbehaves. The misbehavior goes on unabated. Finally, after days of continued misbehavior, the teacher realizes that the actual reward for the child's misbehavior is the laughing and attention the child is getting from his classmates. To reduce the behavior she must recruit the help of the other children, and have them ignore the child's misbehaviors.

The last example shows that we must be careful when looking for the rewards which are responsible for a child's behavior. Sometimes we guess wrong and all we can do is try something else.

CONTROL AND REBELLION

The most common mistakes parents make when using rewards are: (1) trying to use as a reward something the child is not interested in, and (2) inadequately specifying the behavior to be changed. The parents do not necessarily have to tell the child what behavior they are attempting to change, but they should have a very clear idea of what they want to do. If a parent keeps changing his mind, he will, at best, confuse the child and, at worse, goof up the program so that the child becomes a very unwilling participant.

Another mistake commonly made by parents using reward programs is that they do not discuss the program with their children. This is especially important with older children. Imagine this situation: A parent, after reading about the use of rewards, decides to change one of his child's behaviors. The behavior selected by the parent is the child's backtalking behavior. At dinner that night, the parent announced to the family, "I'm going to change Mike's constant backtalking. Each day, if Mike doesn't backtalk, I'm going to give him a dime." Mike is a thirteen-year-old boy.

Mike was embarrassed by his father's discussing the problem in front of the family and mad because he doesn't feel that he is backtalking to his father. He feels that his father makes unreasonable demands on him and doesn't allow him to do things the other boys his age do. For example, Mike's father ordered him to get his hair cut and Mike felt not only that his hair was shorter than the hair of most of the other boys in school, but that his father was being unreasonable. He told his father so and his father slapped him for backtalking.

In a situation like this, the use of rewards might not produce what the father wants. In fact, it may produce just the opposite effect, Mike may deliberately backtalk more than before. He might think, "This is stupid. I'm not going to be treated like a child." Mike is rebelling against his father's program of rewards by increasing his aggressive talk. He is trying to exert some control over the situation.

People who have worked with children and used reward programs have sometimes had this experience when learning how to use rewards. The person using the rewards is making blatant use of his position to control the behavior of the child without the child having any choice in the matter. When this happens, it is not unusual to have the child try to exert countercontrol in the form of defiance or aggression.

The problem of countercontrol can often be prevented if the parent remembers that a program of rewards should be fair. Fairness can often mean letting the child help decide how the program should be set up, the behaviors that should be worked on, and the rewards the child should receive for engaging in the appropriate behaviors. Other times, the problem is not the tasks or the rewards that produce the defiance, but the fact that the child feels he has no choice in the matter and that what is being imposed on him is unjust. Sometimes just discussing the problem with the child will allow the parent to find out why the child is behaving as he is, and the parent may even find that the child is willing to change as long as he has a role in devising the change program.

When setting up reward programs with children, a parent should try to discuss what he is doing, and why he feels it necessary and ask for the child's input. Maybe the child can help devise a better program. A child who has an opportunity to help devise the program will feel he has had some choice in the decision and that the parent isn't just maliciously tring to manipulate his behavior. A child who feels he is being wrongly manipulated is often likely to rebel and intentionally do the opposite of what you want him to do.

CONCLUSIONS

When a parent consistently uses a good and fair program of rewards, several nice things start happening. First, the relationship between the parent and child generally improves. The parent finds that he doesn't have to yell at his children as often, and the child begins modeling the parent's positive behavior. It is fun to hear a child say things such as "Gee, Mom, it's sure fun to talk to you." When the parent acts positively, the child is almost automatically trapped into using more positive ways of interacting with his parents, his siblings, and his friends.

A second nice by-product of a parent's use of rewards is the effect on what might be called the child's self-concept. Because the parent says nice things to the child, he acts as if he is an ok person. The child will also begin to use positive self-rewards, which can be very important later when he enters school and finds that the people around him might not be as rewarding as his parents.

Most rewards are inexpensive, and the effects they have on creating a positive environment for both parent and child make the expense almost trivial. Using rewards will pay good dividends in the more enjoyable relationship a parent will have with his child.

EXAMPLE 7.1

*A Simple Teaching Program
for Children Who Wet the Bed*

Teaching a child to not wet the bed has presented problems for many parents. It is not unusual to hear reports of children who are in their early teens who are still wetting the bed. Bed wetting often causes the child to feel bad and the parents to become overconcerned with their child. A new program for training children to not wet the bed was described by Dr. H. D. Kimmel and his associates. The program is based on the idea that many children who wet the bed do not have adequate bladder capacity to make it through the night. Kimmel's program is designed to increase the amount of urine that a child can store. This procedure can be used by parents. Basically, the parents talk to the child and explain that they want to help the child stop wetting the bed. The parent instructs the child to report each time during the day that he has to urinate. When the child reports, the parent say, "OK, now try to hold it for five minutes before you go to the bathroom." If the child can't tell time, the parent can show the child where the minute hand on the clock must reach before he is to go to the toilet. After the child is able to "hold off" for five minutes, the time is lengthened to ten minutes, then to fifteen minutes. Before long, the child is progressively able to withhold for longer and longer periods of time. The bladder is being trained to store more urine! This is seen at night because the child eventually has more dry nights.

Two things parents can do to increase the effectiveness of this program is to encourage the child to drink fluids during the day. The more fluid the child drinks, the more opportunities he will have to practice delaying going to the bathroom. The second thing the parent should do is reward the child each time he is able to successfully withhold going to the bathroom for the designated time. In addition, special rewards should be arranged for the child if he is able to go through the night without wetting the bed.

From H. D. Kimmel and Ellen Kimmel, An Instrumental Conditioning Method for the Treatment of Enuresis. *Journal of Behavior Therapy and Experimental Psychiatry*, 1970, Vol. 1, pp. 121–123.

EXAMPLE 7.2

Changing Behavior by Not Rewarding It

It is surprising how many of a child's inappropriate behaviors are unintentionally maintained by parents. Parents, by attempting to help a child with a problem, sometimes do just the opposite of what should be done, and end up encouraging the behavior. This was demonstrated in a case study by Dr. Montrose Wolf and his associates. They were presented with a case of a young, retarded girl who vomited frequently. The girl was in a class for the retarded and almost daily would, for no apparent reason, vomit all over herself and anyone or thing in her immediate area. Prior to inviting Wolf and his associates to help with the child's problem, the girl had been checked by the institution's physician who could not find a medical reason for the girl's vomiting behavior.

After observing several sequences when the girl would vomit, Wolf concluded that the teachers' attention—taking the girl from the classroom and changing her clothes— was maintaining the behavior. To test this idea he instructed the teachers not to remove the girl from the class following a vomiting episode. For the first few days this was tried, the rate of vomiting increased greatly, but the girl was required to wear her soiled clothes until the end of the period. Vomiting episodes them became less frequent until the girl was no longer vomiting in class.

The increase in vomiting was expected: when rewards are no longer given for a behavior, there is often a brief increase in the behavior before it begins to decrease.

From M. Wolf, J. Birnbraurer, J. Lawler, and T. Williams, The Operant Extinction, Reinstatement, and Re-extinction of Vomiting Behavior in a Retarded Child. In R. Ulrich, T. Stachnik, and J. Mabry (Eds.), *Control of Human Behavior: From Cure to Prevention.* Glenview, Ill: Scott, Foresman, 1970. Pp. 146–148.

EXERCISE

Use instructions whenever possible to help in teaching your child. Instructions can, if used properly, tell the child precisely what to do, when to do the behavior, and how to do the behavior. An interesting and effective use of instructions is *rules*. Although most of us use rules, we use them only in an informal fashion. Rules can be more effectively used if you follow a few simple guidelines:

1. *Rules should be specific.* That is, they should state precisely what is desired. For example, if you wish to have your child clean her room each day, you may state this as follows: "Sharon will clean her room each morning before eight. The bed must be neatly made, clothes must be picked up, and all toys and books must be placed on the shelves." This set of rules specifies all the important things to be done and when they are to be done.

2. *Rules should be as brief as possible.* If your child is young, complex and wordy rules will only confuse her. A good rule states only what is to be done, how it is to be done, and when it is to be done. Sometimes the rule might also include the reward for following the rule, but other information—especially moralizing—should not be included.

3. *Rules should be repeated frequently.* When you are first trying to improve your child's behavior you should review the rules daily. In the above example, the mother might go over the rules with her daughter every morning. When discussing the rules it should be done in a friendly, encouraging manner. Another way of making the rules known would be to write them on a piece of paper and post them in a conspicuous place.

4. *Rules should be stated in the positive.* For example, a negative case would be: "If the room isn't picked up, Sharon will not be allowed to play outside." The better, more positive case is "If the room is picked up, then Sharon can play outside."

5. *Rules should be fair.* Rules should specify behaviors that are reasonable to expect from a child. For example, I think it is unfair to ask a child to study for two hours immediately after getting home from school. Let the child clear her head and play for a while. Then, if two hours' study are necessary, they can be requested.

Try using a few simple rules to prompt the behaviors you desire from your child. If the rules are used as suggested above, you will have the beginnings of a good program. Note, however, that *rules alone will not produce long-lasting changes. The behavior specified by the rules must be rewarded to produce long-lasting effects.*

8

Providing Cues For Positive Behavior

We are constantly seeing things, listening to sounds, smelling odors, and touching things. These things that stimulate our senses are called *stimuli* and can have interesting effects on our behavior. Let's look at two examples of these effects. Suppose you had just been baking cookies. Your child comes home from school, walks into the kitchen, and a big smile comes on his face. "Wow, Mom, what smells so good?" At another time your small child is walking with you and a large dog comes from behind a house and barks loudly. Your child becomes frightened and starts to cry. What has happened in these situations?

When we carefully look at each situation we see that important stimuli had dramatic effects on the children's behavior. In the first place, the smell of the cookies caused the child to smile and to ask what smelled so good. The smells caused positive reactions by the child. In the second example, the sound and sight of the large dog caused the child to act frightened and to cry. These stimuli produced negative reactions.

Stimuli that are constantly bombarding our sense organs are partly responsible for causing us to behave in predictable ways. Sometimes stimuli cue positive reactions and other times they cue negative reactions. Advertising agencies have made use of this simple concept. If they wish to sell a product, they wrap it in an attractive box, give it an appealing name, and advertise it. Notice how often merchandise is advertised using a child, an attractive woman, or a pet. Advertising people know these things are going to increase the appeal of their product. Using this knowledge of how stimuli influence behavior, advertisers induce people to buy things they neither need nor—before seeing the advertisement—want. Other people, however, try to make more desirable use of their knowledge of how stimuli influence behavior. A person who is writing a book for children who are just beginning to read will include pictures to make the book more interesting and to provide a framework that helps the child understand the words more easily. A psychotherapist will also try to make maximum use of relevant stimuli to help his client improve his behavior. For example, a psychotherapist working with a person who is very unsure of himself might pretend or role-play a situation where he is the client's boss and have his client practice reacting to the authority. The client, in this situation, can be taught to react more appropriately to the stimuli presented by an authority.

The above are examples of how people intentionally use stimuli to influence certain behaviors. Most of the time, however, no one plans how stimuli affect our behavior and we learn this quite by accident. Let's look at how stimuli influence our behavior. Our knowledge can then be used for effective and intentional management of stimuli to help cue the kinds of behavior we want from our children.

HOW STIMULI INFLUENCE BEHAVIOR

When we talk about a stimulus influencing our behavior, what do we mean? Do we react automatically and behave in reflexive ways whenever we encounter a given stimulus? Or is our behavior less automatic? Both are true in certain situations. Sometimes we do react to certain stimuli automatically and without thinking. And it is a good thing to do. For example, we immediately withdraw our hand from a hot stove. If we didn't do this automatically we would suffer bad burns. Our reactions to many stimuli that could cause damage to our bodies require no thought. Our nervous systems are set up to automatically react to these stimuli. This doesn't mean that we can't override this automatic reaction. Sometimes we can, as evidenced by someone who enters a burning building to save his children. The automatic reaction would be to get away from the fire, but we can command ourselves to override these basic reflexes by giving ourselves other cues. In fact, many of the important stimuli in our lives are provided by our thoughts and our emotions.

At other times, when we talk about a stimulus influencing behavior, what is being referred to is the fact that people, in the presence of certain stimuli, are more *likely* to behave in one way rather than another. This isn't an automatic process, but one that is learned by interacting with people or things. For example, a man playing cards with his friends might swear and tell dirty stories, but at a church reception he is very unlikely to do these things. Why? He has learned that certain behaviors are appropriate in certain settings but not in others. In other words, the setting influences his behavior. We can think of many similar examples which show that we are more or less likely to do and say certain things depending upon the situation or occasion. For example, we are more likely to think of food when we are in a restaurant than when we are in the shower. Again, the setting exerts some influence over our thoughts and actions. I'm using the phrase *influencing behavior* in the technical sense to mean that most of our behavior reliably occurs only in the presence of appropriate stimuli. By and large, this is to our advantage. In fact, in most cases it is a good thing that we react in a constant fashion to the stimuli about us. Think of how much time and energy would be wasted if we had to think how we should act in each setting. Life would be unnecessarily complex. The problem is that sometimes stimuli influence inappropriate behaviors, and we must help the child learn to behave in the presence of appropriate stimuli.

In the examples we've looked at, it is rather obvious that we behave differently in different situations, but we can generally guess at the reasons for our behavior. There are other times, however, when the stimuli influencing our behavior are less obvious. A good example of this is the person who has what some psychologists call "free-floating anxiety." This person feels anxious but doesn't know why. He is unaware of the stimuli that are triggering his anxiety. But the result is as real as if he were aware of what it is that is causing the anxiety. What this means is that our behavior is determined by the stimuli that are around us, but we are aware of only some of the stimuli that are influencing our behavior. This is neither good nor bad by itself. Sometimes it is unimportant to be aware of all of the stimuli that influence our behavior. For example, a golfer might be unnecessarily distracted if he were to think about all of the cues that are influencing his golf swing. Because things are going well, he simply ignores the cues. If his swing should start giving him problems, he will then become concerned and seek the help of a professional who can help him locate the stimuli that are causing his problem.

The same type of situation arises for many people in other aspects of life. Sometimes a person will seek the help of other professionals to help find out why he is behaving as he is. He will, in other words, ask a professional to help him find out what stimuli are influencing the behaviors of concern. A child who is having problems reading may ask his teacher to help him, and a child who is afraid of the dark may ask his parents to help him.

Discrimination Learning:
Different Settings, Different Behaviors

How do stimuli come to exert controlling influence over our behavior? Let's look at an example of a child who gets excited whenever his uncle Ed comes to the house. When the child was very small his reaction to Ed might have been one of fear, avoidance, or perhaps indifference. This is not uncommon. Many young children act bashful in the presence of strangers. Uncle Ed likes children, however, and whenever he would arrive he would have a little toy or piece of candy for the child. After a while the child began to approach Ed, and Ed would smile and give the child the treat. It didn't take long for the child to warm up to Ed, and as soon as Ed would arrive the child would be in his lap. Ed had become a stimulus indicating that the child would have fun and maybe get a treat. How had Ed become a positive stimulus for the child's happiness? What had happened is that the child had learned to associate the presence of Ed with pleasant experiences. In the preceding chapter on rewards we found that when a child is rewarded for a behavior he will repeat the behavior more often in the future. The discussion of stimuli and how they influence behavior is a refinement of this concept. When a child is rewarded for some behavior, he usually doesn't do that behavior more frequently in all situations. Usually he is more likely to repeat the behavior only in situations that are the same or similar to the situations in which he was rewarded. Typically, a child who has been rewarded for saying "please" and "thank you" at the dinner table is more likely to repeat these words the next time he is at the table, but he probably will not say "please" when he is getting ready for bed. When a child is rewarded for a behavior in one setting but not others, we call this *discrimination learning.* If a child is learning a discrimination, he is learning that if in certain settings he engages in some behavior, he will be rewarded. If he engages in the behavior in other settings, he might not be rewarded; in fact, he might be punished. An example of this is a child who is learning to box. He will be rewarded for hitting others when he is in the ring and has boxing gloves on, but society is likely to punish him if he hits people when he is not in the ring.

For a child to learn a discrimination he must be rewarded for a behavior in the presence of some stimuli, but not in the presence of other stimuli. After several occasions of this, his behavior is likely to occur in the presence of the stimuli that were present when his behavior was rewarded. He will also be unlikely to engage in the behavior in the presence of stimuli that were not associated with rewards. Let's look at an elaborate example of discrimination training that goes on with most children. Suppose that we were asked to teach several children from a ghetto area to talk more frequently. When we first began to work with these children, they were very uncommunicative. They talked infrequently, and when they did talk they used words that were inappropriate. What could we do? Well, the first thing we would do is reward the children for any talking. Let's suppose we did this and we created talking monsters: they talked constantly. This obviously is inappropriate. Sometimes they should be quiet so that we can teach them other, new concepts. How can we teach the children to discriminate times that are appropriate to talk and times that are inappropriate? This was an actual problem faced by several teachers. They solved the problem in an interesting way. They used what they called a "talk box." When they wanted the children to talk freely they put a blue box on the table in front of the children. When they wanted the children to be silent they removed the box. If the children were talking when the box was on the table they gave the children pieces of candy. When they removed the box the children only received candy when they were silent.[1] This example has obvious

implications for children in other situations. For
who is concerned with his child's constant talking
might wish to try a similar approach to teacl
discriminate when and where it is appropriate to t
where it is appropriate to be silent.

The example of teaching ghetto children demonstr
quirements for teaching a child to respond in the pr   ...am
stimuli and not to respond in the presence of others. Children learn to
discriminate when behavior is appropriate and when it isn't by being
rewarded for the behavior in the presence of appropriate stimuli and
by not being rewarded in the presence of stimuli signaling the behavior
is inappropriate.

Generalization Learning:
Appropriate Behavior in Similar Settings

The opposite of discrimination is *generalization*. Sometimes we
want to teach our children to do things only at certain times and in certain places. When we do this, we are teaching them a discrimination.
Other times we wish to teach the child to do a behavior in many situations where he may only be doing it in certain situations. For example,
you may have noticed that your child is perfectly behaved at home,
but when you go visiting he behaves terribly. What you would like to
do is to teach him to generalize his good behavior which occurs at
home to other settings. To do this, you do the opposite of teaching
your child to discriminate. You reward him for being good in a variety
of settings. The more settings his good behavior is rewarded in, the
more he will generalize to new settings.

Problems in Learning a Discrimination

So far, we have seen that either a child can be taught to perform a
behavior in only one set of stimulus conditions or we can teach him to
generalize his behavior to many settings, depending upon what we
wish to teach him. In this discussion I have assumed that we are intentionally trying to increase the influence of a stimulus over a child's
behavior. Sometimes, however, we teach a child to discriminate or to
generalize quite by accident. In an earlier chapter I mentioned an example of a child who, because of his parent's inconsistency, had
learned to misbehave or not misbehave according to his parent's

If the parent was in a permissive mood he would encourage his child's behavior, but if the parent was in a stern mood he might punish the child for the same behavior. It was mentioned when giving the example that the child might—if he were lucky—learn to discriminate which mood the parent was in and then behave accordingly. This is a good example of unintentionally teaching a child to discriminate the stimuli signaling when a behavior is or is not appropriate. The parent didn't intend to teach his child to "read" his moods; the learning took place quite accidently. This example is very instructive. A child will associate certain stimuli with certain behaviors even if he is not intentionally taught this relationship.

Because this concept is important, let's look at another example of how we might unwittingly teach a child an inappropriate discrimination. Let's suppose that your child came to you when you were busy and said, "Mom, Johnny said that girls are not as smart as boys. Is that true?" Because you were busy and didn't quite hear what your child said you mumbled, "Uh-huh." The child might leave with an erroneous idea of differences between boys and girls. Remember, one of the functions of a reward is feedback. You gave the child feedback that Johnny's statement was correct. Later, you might wonder where your child got such silly information. If she had asked you, you certainly wouldn't have told her that girls are less intelligent than boys.

A child's behavior can come under the influence of many types of stimuli. Some stimuli will influence behavior we might consider appropriate and other stimuli will influence inappropriate behavior. Our knowledge of how stimuli influence behavior can allow us to more effectively manage a child's environment so that we can increase the cues for good behavior and reduce the effectiveness of cues that influence inappropriate behavior.

MANAGING STIMULI
TO PRODUCE APPROPRIATE BEHAVIOR

When you observe your child engaging in inappropriate behaviors one of the first things you should do is try to find out which stimuli are controlling the behavior. We can sometimes find out about the stimuli by talking to our children as described in Chapter 2. Other times we can locate the stimuli by observing the conditions present when the child behaves inappropriately. You might find, for example, that your child is noisy and acts "wild" only when certain of his friends are visiting him. When other friends are visiting, his behavior is much more appropriate; they play and enjoy themselves without tearing up the house. What stimuli differ when the different friends are visiting? You may find that your child plays different games when different friends are visiting. With friends that produce the wild, noisy behavior your child might play cops and robbers—an active game. With the quieter friends your child might spend more time coloring and looking through books. Here you have an idea of the stimuli influencing your child's behavior. It might not be that his friends are bad and noisy, but that your child has learned to play in one way with some friends and another way with other friends. The different friends are stimuli influencing different play behaviors.

Once you have found the stimuli which influence the child's behavior, you can then consider ways of rearranging the stimuli to increase the likelihood that your child will engage in appropriate play behavior when both sets of friends are visiting. One way of handling the situation in our example would be to make available cues for quiet play when the children who cue noisy behavior come to visit. For example, you might wish to bring out puzzles, coloring books, and so forth and tell the children, including your child, you have a surprise for them if they can put a puzzle together or color a picture. After they have been playing for a few minutes you might give them a cookie. Now that you have rewarded the children for playing quietly, you might wish to have them go outside and play. What you are trying to teach the children is that play in the house should be quiet. Outside play can be noisier. After several repetitions of arranging quiet toys and rewarding the children for playing quietly for a few minutes, the children will learn to associate the house with quiet play. You have rearranged cues or stimuli to produce a more desirable play in the house—a good example of managing stimuli which influence a child's behavior.

Now that we've looked at a general example of how we can effectively manage the stimuli influencing a child's behavior, let's look at some specific techniques of how to change the way in which stimuli influence behavior. For purposes of illustration, I will show how specific procedures can be used to change the influence that stimuli have over inappropriate behavior.

Stimulus Substitution

Sometimes the problem we have with a child is that stimuli which are currently influencing the child's behavior are not those we would prefer. To illustrate, let's look at an example of a child who forgets to flush the toilet after using it. Each time the child goes to the bathroom the parent has to ask, "Did you flush the toilet?" Typically the child hasn't, and the parent sends the child back to finish the job, which he does when reminded. The problem here is not that the child doesn't do the behavior, but that the child must be reminded each time. In other words, the stimulus influencing flushing is not the completion of going to the bathroom, but the parent's request. What the parent would like is the child upon completion of the toileting act to flush the toilet. The parent's task is to substitute completing the toilet act for the parental request as the effective stimulus influencing flushing. How can this be done? One way would be to use the positive practice overcorrection procedure described in the chapter on punishment. The parent would go into the bathroom each time the child completed her toilet and, if the child failed to flush, the parent would have the child engage in positive practice of going into the bathroom, pulling her underpants down, sitting on the toilet, getting off the toilet, pulling up her clothes, and flushing the toilet. The child may be made to positive-practice four or five times after each time when she did not flush after toileting. When the child correctly flushes the toilet the parent should reward the child, even if it is just with praise. After several repetitions of positive practice for mistakes, and of rewards for correct flushing, the stimulus of getting off the toilet will effectively encourage flushing. What the parent will have done is to substitute one stimulus for another to influence flushing the toilet.

Stimulus substitution can be an important procedure to help a child learn to respond to correct stimuli when the behavior already occurs but is under the influence of incorrect stimuli. Another common example of substituting a more appropriate stimulus for an inappropriate one is in the area of language training. For example, a child might incorrectly label a cow with the word "horse." Here, the stimulus of a cow is causing the child to say the incorrect response, "horse." The parent, to correct the stimulus for the child's saying "horse," might show the child a series of pictures of horses and cows and reward the child for correctly labeling each animal.

Changing the Function of a Stimulus

Sometimes the problem is one where a stimulus influences an inappropriate response such as fear. Because of the situation, the parent doesn't want to substitute another stimulus to reduce the child's fear, but to reduce the child's fear response to that stimulus. In other words, what we want is for the child to behave differently in the presence of a stimulus and to find out how we might change the value of the stimulus and therefore change the child's behavior in response to the stimulus. For our example, let's imagine a child, while playing on the school playground, saw another child fall from the monkey bars and hurt himself. The hurt child began bleeding, screaming, and fell down several times while trying to get into the school building. Our child saw this happen and was very frightened. By the time she got home from school that night she was in a complete panic. During the night she had nightmares and upon awaking the next morning refused to go to school. When her mother told her she was acting silly, the girl began to cry. Her fear of school was very obvious.

How could we reduce the girl's fear of school? One procedure that has been very effective for reducing fears is called *systematic desensitization.* This technique works very similar to the way a physician might reduce your sensitivity to an allergen (allergy-producing substance). The physician gives you an injection of a very small amount of the allergen, and your body builds up a defense against that dosage. By progressively giving you larger doses of the allergen, your body becomes capable of warding off any ill effects. If the treatment works, you will eventually no longer have an allergic reaction to natural allergens. In systematic desensitization we arrange conditions which reduce a child's fear and then progressively expose the child to stimuli that are more and more likely to evoke a fear response; because the child has been exposed to weak stimuli without reacting fearfully, he will be unlikely to react with fear to slightly stronger stimuli.

In our example we might want to talk to the child and explain that, although there is no reason to be afraid of school, we recognize that she is and we would like to help her get rid of her fear. After we have explained what we want to do, we would encourage her to walk with us toward the school. At first we might only go halfway. The next day we might go even further. It might take several days before she can walk to the schoolyard without being fearful. Then we may want to have her only go into the schoolhouse on the first day she reaches school. Each day she may go for a longer and longer period of time.

By systematically exposing the child to the fear stimulus, we can reduce her fear. If we expose her to the fear-producing stimuli too rapidly, we might increase the fear. By watching the child we can observe when she starts to show fear and then we can stop our progress until she can comfortably handle that step. One way of increasing the speed with which we can reduce the fear is by rewarding the child for reaching each new step. The child should be praised for each improvement in her ability to cope with the fear.

The progressive exposure to a fear stimulus, especially when each new step is rewarded, can be used to reduce a child's fearful reactions to many things. How might you, for example, reduce your child's fear of the dark using the procedure of systematic desensitization? One way would be to get a rheostat (light-dimming switch) for the child's bedroom light and each night progressively reduce the intensity of the light. If the steps are small enough, the child will have less and less fear until he is able to sleep in the room without a light. What other examples of children's fears might systematic desensitization be used for?

Another way of reducing a child's inappropriate reaction to a given stimulus is to present the stimulus at full intensity but make sure the effect of the stimulus is reduced because of other things you do. This procedure can be used to reduce a child's aggressive reactions to being teased, for example. Let's suppose you are working with a child who "blows up" every time someone says something derogatory to him. You've noticed that he gets especially mad and hits out at people if they call him names. Because of this reaction, some of the local bullies have intentionally provoked the child into fights. Your problem is how to get the child to stop acting aggressively whenever teased and to just ignore those teasing him. How could you go about this? A psychologist working in a school for delinquent boys handled this problem nicely. He would call one of the boys who reacted inappropriately to taunts into his office and explain to the boy why the behavior was inappropriate: it got him into fights, it made the school staff unhappy with him, and it was making the boy unhappy. The psychologist then told the boy that whenever he saw the boy in the halls he was going to intentionally taunt him by saying the very things that made him angry. But he wasn't going to do it to make the boy angry, but rather to help the boy learn to react in more positive ways. At first, the psychologist said he would tell the boy beforehand that he was going to say something the boy disliked, then when the boy was ready, he would say it. So when the psychologist saw the boy he would walk up to the boy and say, "John, are you ready for a barb?" Then he would say something that would normally make the child angry, but because the boy knew it wasn't intended to be rude or mean he wouldn't react with anger. When the boy was capable of controlling his anger, the psychologist progressively reduced the warning that he was "barbing" the boy. For example, the psychologist might just walk up to the boy and, with a smile on his face, call the boy a name. Step by step the boy was learning to respond appropriately to barbs.

Both systematic desensitization and "barbing" are ways of changing a child's inappropriate reaction to stimuli by changing the influence each stimulus has over the behavior of a child. Although we may have done similar things with our children in the past, you can see that effective use of these procedures, as with most of the other procedures described in the book, requires thought and planning to be most effective. Care should be taken not to proceed too quickly using these procedures. An unnecessary goof might have a negative effect on your progress.

Fading

Sometimes when you want your child to learn some behavior it is easier to teach the behavior in the presence of a very dominant stimulus even though you may not want that stimulus to influence the behavior later. This is done when the dominant stimulus will facilitate learning and when the behavior learned in the presence of the dominant stimulus can be later shifted to a more desirable stimulus. Let's look first at an example of how this might be done when we are trying to teach a child how to tell time; later we will consider how the same procedure can be used to reduce the frequency of an undesirable behavior.

Young children often have difficulty learning to tell time because the numbers of the face of the clock mean two things, hours and minutes. One way of quickly teaching a child to tell time would be to make a cardboard clock with the hour hand one color and the minute hand another color. Then we would make numbers representing hours the same color as the hour hand. We would also make a second set of numbers which represents minutes. These numbers would be the same color as the minute hand. This clock provides the child with cues which he wouldn't find on normal clocks, but these exaggerated cues facilitate learning to tell time. When the child can reliably tell time with the exaggerated cues, we can begin to "fade out" the exaggerated cues and "fade in" the stimuli found on normal clocks. For example, the first step might be to make the hands of the clock the same color so that the child learns to respond to hand size rather than hand color. Again, when the child is reliably telling time with hands of the same color, we can make the number representing the minutes and hours the same color. Eventually, we start fading out the numbers representing the minutes. By doing this slowly, the child is able to fill in the missing numbers. As more and more minute numbers are faded out he will be learning to respond to the numbers that are still available on the clock.

As you can see, fading represents a way of teaching a child by maximizing cues and later slowly withdrawing cues so that the child is responding to the appropriate ones. The advantage of using stimuli that are exaggerated is that we increase the likelihood that the child will learn the behavior in a shorter time and without making many mistakes. Sometimes when a child makes mistakes he isn't provided with feedback that his behavior is inaccurate and he may persist with the incorrect behavior. A good example of this is the language mistakes that children make that are not corrected. A child may for example, say the past tense of *to give* as "gived" rather than "gave." The longer the child persists with the incorrect word the more difficult it will be to change. Another reason we should encourage learning with few errors is because sometimes children get upset when they are incorrect. The evidence indicates that learning without errors is every bit as persistent as learning with mistakes. But learning without errors reduces the emotional upset associated with mistakes.

The fading procedure can be used to change the cues influencing other behaviors. Sometimes a child engages in some behavior that is appropriate and desirable, but the stimuli that are influencing the behavior are not the most desirable ones. Let's suppose that you have a child who soils his pants. The behaviors of evacuating the bowels and bladder are desirable, but the cues controlling the behavior are not. What you would like to do is to maintain the behavior, but change the stimuli influencing the behavior. One way of doing this would be to bring the eliminating behavior under the influence of some very conspicuous stimulus such as a buzzer and then later shift to a more appropriate stimuli. Drs. Azrin and Foxx have described such a procedure. They took children who soiled their pants and fitted them with special "toilet alarm" underpants. These underpants had small wires attached to two snaps in the bottom of the underpants. Whenever the child began to void, the moisture of the urine or fecal matter would close an electrical circuit between the snaps and trigger off a small buzzer attached to a belt around the child's waist. As soon as the parent heard the buzzer she would rush the child to the toilet where the child would finish eliminating. When the child eliminated in the toilet, the parent would reward the child. After a while, the child began to respond to the tension on the bladder or bowel and go to the toilet before the buzzer sounded.

In this example, the stimuli originally influencing the child's behavior are difficult to determine. It might have been the need to eliminate, the feel of the underpants, and so on. Because of the difficulty in using the existing stimuli, Azrin and Foxx brought going to the toilet under the influence of a very conspicuous stimulus, the buzzer. Then the mother shifted to a more appropriate stimulus when the buzzer sounded. She did this by rewarding the child for eliminating in the toilet.[2]

As we have seen in this section, a parent can use knowledge of how stimuli influence behavior to change inappropriate behavior. The examples we've looked at have generally been concerned with attempts to alter some important behavior, but the same ideas can be used for more commonly occurring situations. Let's look at several examples of how we already use stimulus-influencing procedures with our children and how we might use them more effectively to increase the positiveness of the relationship between parent and child.

USING STIMULUS-INFLUENCING CONCEPTS TO IMPROVE PARENT-CHILD RELATIONSHIPS

If a child is behaving appropriately, his parents are happy; if the child is acting inappropriately, his parents often get mad and react negatively toward the child. This in turn makes the child unhappy.

[2]Azrin, N.H. and Foxx, R.M. *Toilet Training in Less Than a Day*. New York: Simon and Schuster, 1974.

Many times we can avert these problems and hard feelings between ourselves and our children by taking the time to arrange an environment that is more likely to encourage appropriate behaviors. Often these stimuli that we arrange can totally prevent inappropriate behavior from occurring. Other times the stimuli are effective in disrupting the inappropriate behaviors and encouraging a change to more appropriate behaviors. Whichever the case, the fewer confrontations between parent and child about a child's inappropriate behaviors, the happier the relationship will be. It makes sense to spend a few minutes that are required to arrange stimuli to encourage positive behaviors. Let's look at some ways in which this can be done.

Frowns and Facial Expressions

What do you do if you observe your child doing something you feel he shouldn't be doing? Many of us will frown, shake our heads, and show disgust. What are we doing? Aren't we trying to provide stimuli that indicate our disapproval? When we think of frowns and so on as stimuli which are intended to influence our child's behavior, we can begin to consider how these stimuli might affect the behavior of the child and how we can more effectively use these cues. For example, let's look at the influence exerted by a frown. When we frown at a child what we might be signaling to the child is "If you don't stop doing that, I will be very mad and I might punish you." Sometimes this works, but very often the stimuli are simply not strong enough to influence the child's behavior. In this situation we may end up punishing the child. If the frown had been effective, the parent's reaction might not have been so severe. And the child would certainly feel better about the way things turned out.

A research study has shown that the negative attention of frowning combined with other actions of the parent can be made to be very effective for influencing a child's behavior if it is used correctly. The psychologists doing the research study had teachers compare the punishment technique of isolation (removing the child from the situation for a few minutes) with an exaggerated showing of displeasure. Displeasure was shown to the child by the teacher frowning and leaning slightly forward in the direction of the child. The teacher held the pose for about ten seconds without saying a word. The results of the research study showed the "negative attention" of frowning and staring at the child was every bit as effective as punishing the child using isolation. The obvious advantage of negative attention over punishment is that negative attention can be delivered immediately following the child's inappropriate behavior. Besides this advantage, children often get upset when punishment procedures are used. By using negative attention before the child has had time to complete the inappropriate behavior we can sometimes terminate the child's misbehavior before it has reached a point where we feel he must be punished. And since punishment often has effects that are undesirable, we are more likely not to produce unnecessary emotional reactions in the child.

Instructions

Another very common use of stimuli to influence our children's behavior is through the use of instructions. When we say to a child, "Mary, please pick up your coat," what are we hoping to accomplish? Aren't we intending the instruction to act as a stimulus influencing Mary's picking up her coat? In this sense, instructions act as stimuli to influence a child's behavior. In Chapter 3, "Talking with Your Children: Helping to Solve Problems," I mentioned that instructions can be very effective for influencing behavior. The effectiveness depends on several things. First, the more complete the instructions, the more likely the child's behavior will be carried out correctly. Secondly, when the child correctly responds to the instructions, he should be rewarded. The rewards will increase the likelihood that the next time the child's parents give him instructions he will follow them. When parents complain that their children won't listen to what they tell them (instructions), the problem is usually one of three things. First, the instructions were too vague and the child didn't understand what the parent was asking of him. Or second, the child is never rewarded for following instructions and because following instructions doesn't pay off, he simply quits. The third reason a child might not follow his parents' instructions is because the child perceives the instructions as unfair. For example, a parent might say to the older of two girls, "Mary, don't make Sally cry. Let her play with the doll." Because Mary was playing with the doll first, she may rebel and not obey the parent's instructions.

If a parent follows a few simple rules, instructions can be used to effectively influence a child's behavior. Some of the basic rules are:

1. Use as few instructions as necessary to accomplish what is desired. If a parent gives too many instructions, the child might just become confused.

2. Be consistent in the wording of instructions.

3. Instructions should be as short and simple as possible. Long, detailed instructions will again confuse the child.

4. With young children, or children who have problems understanding instructions, include only one activity per instruction. In other words, a parent shouldn't give an instruction that says, "Do A, then B, then C." These elaborate instructions might be difficult for the child to remember.

5. Make sure the instruction specifies a behavior (and sometimes the consequence). As an example, a parent should say, "Put the plate down," rather than, "Do as I tell you."

6. If a child engages in the instructed behavior, he should be rewarded, even if it is only by having the parent say "thank you."

7. Finally, instructions can be made more effective if they are part of a positive framework rather than a negative one. For example, a child is much more willing to engage in a behavior if his mother is smiling than if she does not show a positive expression. The reason for this is that the child has probably learned that when the mother is smiling he is more likely to be rewarded for the behavior than when the mother is not smiling.

Routines

It might seem strange to consider a routine as a stimulus, but they can be very effective for reducing problem interactions between parent and child. For example, some parents have trouble getting their children to bed at night. The child doddles and goofs around and the parents often end up yelling at the child. This usually means that the child goes to bed unhappy and the parent shakes his head at the child's noncompliance. Sometimes a bedtime routine can eliminate these problems by acting as a stimulus influencing the child's going to bed. Let's look at an example where parents established a bedtime routine with their small child and completely eliminated any problems with the child going to bed. They told the child that if he would get his clothes off, get into the bathtub, brush his teeth, dress for bed, his father would tell him a story in bed. The child loved stories and quickly completed his bath. After the child was in bedclothes, his father took a glass of juice and a storybook and went into the child's bedroom. The child followed after a few minutes and was given the juice and told the story. After the story, the boy's father kissed his child, turned out the light, and left the room. The boy remained in bed. This routine is still carried on and the child hardly ever complains about going to bed. The routine became a stimulus for getting ready for bed and going to sleep.

Other routines can be equally effective. Sometimes, for example, a parent finds that he has difficulty arranging time for his children. He knows that his relationship with his children would be greatly improved if he could spend more time, but things always seem to come up. An established routine might be the answer to his problem. We are, by and large, creatures of habit. If we set our alarms for 7:00 A.M., we find that after several days we start waking up before the alarm rings. By arranging a schedule we are much more likely to do things than if we do them only when we have time. The same is true of interacting with our children. A father who finds that he is not spending as much time as he would like with his children could set up a schedule where he plays with his children for thirty minutes after dinner. This doesn't sound like much time, and most people would prefer to be more spontaneous in their interactions, but many parents who are concerned with spending more time with their children find this a convenient way of increasing time with their children. The children will probably enjoy the time with their parent, and it is very likely that the parent will also enjoy himself and probably begin spending even more time with his children.

The types of routines discussed above can work because they are not coercive: a child isn't forced into something. The routines work because the stimulus conditions are arranged so that the likelihood of the behavior occurring naturally is greatly increased. Routines that force a child to do something are probably not very rewarding to the child and may not be very fair.

Routines have one drawback: the child develops the expectancy that the parent will follow through with his part in the routine. A parent, for example, who reads his child a story as part of the bedtime routine is expected to do his part. If the parent should stop telling stories, he can foul up the routine and possibly cause the child to distrust his parent. This occurs because routines can be thought of as a chain. Each behavior is a link in the chain signaling the next link. Take one link out and the whole chain might come apart. To avoid this problem, a parent could do two things. First, he could try to insure that his part in the routine is consistent while the routine is being established. Secondly, if a parent cannot fulfill his part, he could explain this to the child. If the parent has been fair, his children will understand.

Preventing Inappropriate Behavior by Providing Cues for Appropriate Behavior

Sometimes children engage in inappropriate behaviors not because they are reacting to stimuli which influence these inappropriate behaviors, but because stimuli influencing other, appropriate behaviors are not present. Imagine this situation: a child is forced to play inside because of the terrible weather outside. After a while the child begins to run about the house or follow his mother around wanting her to entertain him. Why is the child doing this? Is it because stimuli for inappropriate behavior are present? Probably not. The child is probably bored. Boredom can often mean that stimuli for appropriate behaviors are either very weak or not present. When this occurs we can expect the child to become restless and engage in behaviors that are not desirable. How can we prevent this from occurring?

One way of preventing the breakdown in a child's appropriate behavior would be to arrange the environment so as to provide the child with new stimuli that will keep him entertained and acting happy. For example, one mother solved this problem very neatly. Her children, like most children, had more toys than they would play with on a given day. Each week or two the children's mother would spend ten to fifteen minutes going through the children's toys and selecting toys that the children had played with in the past but were not playing with now. She would put these toys up in the top of a closet. Now whenever her children began acting bored she would bring the hidden toys from the closet. The children were ecstatic! It was as if the toys which they hadn't seen for a week or two were brand-new. The children would immediately begin to play with the "new toys," and their boredom would be gone.

Using this simple little idea of "recycling" toys, the mother was able to greatly reduce her children's boredom and, even more importantly, the bad feelings that might have arisen if the children had gotten on her nerves.

There are other ways in which we can enrich the environmental stimuli to increase the likelihood of children engaging in appropriate behaviors. For example, many parents complain that their children don't pick up after themselves. When this happens, parents often resort to yelling at the children. Typically, the child then picks up whatever he left lying about but often does not change his future behavior. He continues to leave things about the house. Dr. Ogden Lindsley, one of the best-known psychologists in the area of child management, once described what he did with his own children in this situation. One night at the dinner table he announced that beginning the next day everything left lying about the house and not in its proper place would be put into a "Sunday box." This large box containing the items left about the house during the week would only be opened on Sunday evening. If, however, something that was very important was put into the box, it could be removed before Sunday only if something of equal value to the person were put in the box in its place. The idea was a great success—in fact, too successful. On the first day that the box was available, Dr. Lindsley left his cigarette lighter lying about and one of his children put it in the box. What was fair for one was fair for all.

Sunday, when it came time to open the box, the family gathered around and had a good time laughing at what was in the box. Everyone, however, had been much more careful to pick up their things.[3]

The Sunday box not only accomplished what was intended— picking up things—but it also encouraged more positive interactions by members of the family. Lindsley had been wise in his way of handling a problem of how to get stimuli to influence appropriate behavior.

These last examples have several things in common: the parent observed an inappropriate behavior and tried to determine which cues were influencing the behavior; the parent tried to arrange cues that would influence behaviors which were more appropriate and incompatible with the undesirable behaviors; and both the parent and child enjoyed the new situation more than when the inappropriate behaviors were occurring. Other problems can be averted by doing a similar analysis of what behavior is occurring, what are the cues in-

[3]Lindsley, O. R. An Experiment with Parents Handling Behavior at Home. *Johnstone Bulletin,* 1966, Vol. 9, pp. 27-36.

fluencing the behavior, and how could cues influencing other, more appropriate behaviors be arranged. How would you, for example, handle this situation? Your child is in bed with a mild case of measles and after a couple of hours becomes bored. He starts yelling, "Mom, come and talk to me," "Mom, I'm thirsty," and so on. You are quite sure he is doing this only because he is bored, and you feel you don't have time to run to him every time he calls. What would you do?

Well, you've probably decided that the child's behavior is occurring because he has few stimuli available which influence positive behavior. Now, what stimuli do influence good behavior? You might decide that one thing which would make the child happy would be to watch television. So you take the TV into his room and tell him, "Let's pretend you are in the hospital. People in the hospital sometimes have a TV in their room. I'll pretend that I'm a nurse and I'll check in on you occasionally, but I have to check with other people, so I can't come in all the time." This game might be a lot of fun for the child and solve the problem of the child's boredom at the same time.

These examples demonstrate that the relationship between parents and children can be enriched without a great expenditure of time and money. Sometimes all that is required is a simple analysis of how and where problem interactions are occurring and rearranging the stimulus environment so as to increase the likelihood of appropriate behaviors. The end result is fewer negative interactions and more positive interactions.

One of the most important stimulus conditions influencing a child's behavior is the behavior of the parent. I've alluded to how a parent's actions can affect a child's behavior, but because of the importance of this concept, the next chapter will be concerned with how children learn to imitate others.

EXAMPLE 8.1

Using Systematic Desensitization With Infants

Most of the teaching techniques described in this book can be used with people of all ages. Systematic desensitization, for example has been used with adults, teenagers, children, and infants. Of course, the specifics of the program will vary with the different age groups. This was nicely demonstrated by

Peter Bentler, who reported a case study showing how systematic desensitization was used with an eleven-month-old girl.

The girl, like most children, enjoyed playing in her wading pool and taking baths. Then one day she slipped and fell while she was in the tub. She began screaming and was obviously very frightened. Afterwards she was not only afraid of the tub, but also of the wading pool, faucets, and water in any part of the house and to being washed in the hand basin.

Treatment of the infant's fear consisted of four parts: First toys were placed in the empty bathtub and the girl was given free access to the bathroom and the toys. During this phase of treatment she would occasionally remove a toy from the tub, but would not remain near the tub. The second stage consisted of sitting the girl on the table near the sink filled with water. Toys were placed in the water and, at first, the girl began to scream, but later played with toys on the table and near the sink. These toys were moved progressively closer to the sink until she was finally entering the sink. This caused a brief bout of crying, but helped to desensitize her to water. The third step consisted of washing the child in the bathroom sink while she was playing with her favorite toy. The child began playing with the mirror and eventually with the water in the sink. During this stage she also began playing with the sprinkler in the yard. Finally, the parents began washing the child in the tub with the water running at diaper-changing time. At first the girl began to cry, but parental hugging and firmness caused her to stop crying after two days. At twelve-and-three-quarters months the child was fully recovered and playing normally around water.

From P. M. Bentler, An Infant's Phobia Treated with Reciprocal Inhibition Therapy. *Journal of Child Psychology and Psychiatry*, 1967, Vol. 3, pp. 185–189.

EXAMPLE 8.2

She Doesn't Talk in School: An Example of the Use of Fading

What can be done with an eleven-year-old girl who has never talked in school? Psychologists R. D. Conrad, J. L. Delk, and C. Williams described such a case. The child had never been known to talk in school either to the teacher or to her classmates. Was the girl mute? Only at school, it appears. When the girl's parents and friends were interviewed, they said that the girl was normal in her talking outside of the classroom. They tried to use a fading procedure. Therapy began with the girl in her own home. A mental health worker went to the girl's home and as part of the procedure had the girl name words presented on flash cards. The flash cards were used as an objective measure of the girl's willingness to talk in the situation. If the girl would name the words on each card, she was considered to be talking in that environment. After the girl was naming the cards at home, the health worker invited a friend to come to the girl's house and had the girl name the cards in the friend's presence. Next, therapy was moved to the mental health clinic where the girl was encouraged to name the cards with just the health worker and a friend present. Next, the teacher and several friends were invited to come to the clinic. Eventually, therapy was moved to the classroom, but with just the teacher and a few friends present. Later the girl performed in front of the whole class. One year after she was still performing normally in the classroom.

This is an excellent example of the use of fading. At first the girl would not speak in front of her teacher or fellow classmates, but would speak to her mother and close friends. Control of speaking was then shifted to a new location (the mental health clinic), but was still in the presence of friends. Finally control of speaking was faded to the classroom. The girl would now talk to her teacher and classmates where she was previously silent.

From R. D. Conrad, J. L. Delk, and C. Williams, The Use of Stimulus Fading Procedure in the Treatment of Situation Specific Mutism: A Case Study. *Journal of Behavior Therapy and Experimental Psychiatry*, 1974, Vol. 5, pp. 99–100.

EXERCISE

Arranging cues for appropriate behaviors rather than trying to eliminate inappropriate behaviors is a good example of positive parenting. The advantages of cueing positive behaviors are several: (a) the inappropriate behavior usually decreases; (b) the child gets practice engaging in a behavior that is more appropriate; and (c) the relationship between parent and child is positive rather than negative—which often occurs when punishment is used.

How should you set up a program using cues for positive behavior? Can any positive behavior be increased? It is probably a good idea not to try to increase just any positive behavior. What you should do is increase a behavior which competes with the undesirable behavior. For example, if your child has a bad habit of whining and complaining each morning before going to school, you should try to cue positive, happy behaviors. A child can't be positive and happy and also whine and complain. Technically, we could say that these particular positive behaviors are incompatible with whining and complaining. This is the ideal when trying to replace an inappropriate behavior with one which is more appropriate—the child should not be able to do both behaviors at the same time.

See if you can develop cues to encourage a behavior which is incompatible with an undesirable behavior in which your child engages. At first, you might wish to approach the problem using the questions I've listed below. They will help determine which behaviors you should try to develop cues for.

1. *What are the circumstances (cues) for the inappropriate behavior?* This is the first question asked when determining which cues are *currently* influencing your child's behavior. You might note if the behavior occurs during certain times of the day, in certain places, or if the behavior only occurs under unusual circumstances. For example, you may find that the inappropriate behavior occurs most often when the child has been up late the night before. In this case, it might be that the child is just tired. Whatever you determine,

the more appropriate behaviors you wish to strengthen should be determined by the cues influencing the current, inappropriate behavior.

2. What behavior does my child enjoy that is incompatible with the inappropriate behavior? The important aspect of this question is to try to identify a behavior that your child engages in—that he enjoys—which is incompatible with the behavior you wish to change.

3. What cues control the more desirable behavior? Here you try to find out under what circumstances the desirable behavior occurs.

4. How can I make the cues which control the desirable behavior occur when the less desirable behavior usually occurs? Although this is the most difficult point, it can usually be handled with a little thought. In our example of the child who whines and complains in the mornings you might have found that he normally is happy when you organize the household in unusual ways. If so, you might try having breakfast outside for several mornings. This unusual situation might cue the kinds of behavior that are desirable.

5. If the appropriate behavior occurred, did I reward it? Once again, remember that the cues simply initiate the behavior. To maintain the desirable behavior it should be rewarded.

9

Children Learn
By Observing
Others

One afternoon I was amusing myself by watching a four-year-old child and his father out for a walk. The father had his hands in his jacket pockets and walked with his head down. Occasionally he kicked at a stone on the sidewalk. Similarly, his four-year-old son had his hands in his pockets, walked with his head down, and occasionally kicked at a stone. It was as if the same person was being represented in two sizes: full size and miniature. Why was there such a striking similarity between the father's actions and those of the child? My guess is that the child was directly imitating his father's actions. The evidence for this was the number of times the child looked over at his father to see if what he was doing matched his dad's actions. If the child observed his father take his hands from his jacket, the boy did the same.

Watching the two was both heartwarming and very instructive. It was heartwarming to see that the child wanted to be like his father. The father and his son probably had a very positive relationship. It was instructive in that the child's imitation of his father's actions

130

showed how very important parents are for providing cues which influence their children's behavior. Our children observe what we do and, if the situation is right, they often repeat our actions. Like it or not, whenever we are around our children, they are learning from us. What our children learn might not be intentionally taught, but they are certainly learning.

Some psychologists such as Albert Bandura, a past president of the American Psychological Association, feel that most of what we learn about our world occurs because of our observing other people.[1] This makes sense. If we had to learn each new behavior by trial and error, we wouldn't be much more advanced than, say, a mouse. In a sense, man has sort of streamlined learning. Rather than having to experience everything directly, we can acquire much of our necessary information and behavior indirectly by watching, hearing, and reading about what others have done. Psychologists call this type of learning by various names, such as imitative learning, observational learning, and vicarious learning. Regardless of what we call it, we obtain a tremendous amount of information and learn ways of behaving by interacting with others and using their experiences to enhance our own competency. But how does observational learning take place? What are the necessary ingredients for us to learn from observing others?

HOW CHILDREN LEARN TO IMITATE

Consider an example of a very young child imitating his mother. This will allow us to look at an example of observational learning and the conditions that are important for the learning to take place. A mother is teaching her one-year-old son to play patty-cake. The mother will generally sit with the child on her lap, hold his hands, and guide them through the clapping and rolling while singing the patty-cake song to the child. After a while the mother doesn't have to guide the child's movements quite as much. She simply performs the behaviors and tells the child, "Play patty-cake." The child's clapping may not be perfectly coordinated, but what does the mother do when her child imitates her actions? Isn't the mother usually delighted? She will hug the baby and kiss him and tell herself what a smart child she

---

[1]Bandura, A. and Walters, R.H. *Social Learning and Personality Development.* New York: Holt, Rinehart and Winston, 1963.

has. (She might also tell everyone else in the neighborhood.) What did the mother do to teach her child?

Let's look at some of the basic components of observational learning. Did the mother reward the child? Yes, her delight and hugs and kisses probably made the child happy—a good sign that the behavior was rewarded. In addition, before the child had learned to imitate the mother, the mother's guiding the child's hands, the closeness of the two, and the singing of the patty-cake song probably were effective rewards for the child's paying attention and letting himself be played with. Yes, in this situation, there are usually plenty of rewards. Certainly enough to increase the child's doing the behavior again with his mother.

What about cues? Did the mother provide stimuli that might eventually influence the child's behavior? Again the answer is yes. The mother held the child, guided his hands, and sang the song. All of these will act as cues increasing the chance that when the mother repeats the cues the child will play patty-cake. With both rewards for the child's behavior and the cues signaling the behavior, the basic ingredients of a teaching situation are present. The child will learn to respond appropriately in the presence of the cues because when he has done so before he has found the situation very rewarding.

Factors Influencing Observation Learning

The basic ingredients for observational learning are stimuli cuing the behavior and rewards for successful completion of the behavior. These basic ingredients are necessary for all learning situations. For observational learning to take place, other conditions are also important. For example, a child is not likely to imitate all people. Some people provide cues that the child is more likely to respond to than the cues provided by others. That is, some people are better models than others. In addition, not all children are equally likely to imitate the behavior of another person. These factors—model characteristics and (child) observer characteristics—are important determinants of how successful we can be in teaching children using observational procedures.

Model Characteristics. What are the characteristics of a good model? Let's think of whom we might imitate. This might give us some insight into what constitutes important model characteristics for a child. Let's suppose you were taking a class in painting at the local community center. During one of the class periods you found you were having trouble with a particular way of using your brush. Whom would you observe to try to find out the correct way of doing the stroke—the teacher, or one of your fellow classmates who seems to be as confused as you are? The teacher, of course. Generally, we tend to model people who have demonstrated competence more than those whom we judge as being less competent. The same is true with children. A child, when he is unsure of how to act in a situation, is likely to observe and imitate someone he thinks knows how to behave appropriately. For example, if you were to take your child and a friend of his to lunch at a posh restaurant and your child was unsure of how to act, he is much more likely to imitate your behavior than that of his friend. At least for a little while. The child does this because he sees you as having more competency in this situation than his friend, whom he might perceive as being as naive as himself.

Perceived competency, then, is one of the most important characteristics of a good model. If we perceive someone as being competent, we will imitate his behavior. If we perceive the person as incompetent, we won't. This little fact can get parents into trouble. A child often thinks his parents know everything about the world. If the child is unsure of how to act, he will observe how his parents handle the situation and then imitate their behavior. Let's look at an example of how this can often produce undesirable behaviors in our children. Imagine a child who observes his father tell an "adult" joke to a group of friends. The friends laugh, rewarding the boy's father for telling the joke. Because the child saw his father tell the joke and make everyone laugh, the boy decides to tell the joke at a later time. But he chooses an audience that is not appropriate for the story, his mother's bridge group. It is highly likely that the boy wouldn't be rewarded for telling the joke. In fact, it is more than likely he will be punished. Later, after apologizing for her son's behavior the mother might ask the child, "What got into you, telling a story like that?" What got into the child was an unfortunate learning experience. Because the child had been rewarded in the past for imitating his father, he generalized to a new situation where he didn't know the ground rules.

This example illustrates an important guideline for parents. Our children will imitate our behavior because they see us as being competent. Sometimes when children imitate behaviors that are situationally inappropriate, we punish them for their misbehavior, a condition that might weaken our power as an effective model for our children. We can prevent this by making sure that our behavior is what we want our child to imitate. If we behave in ways that we don't want our child to imitate, then maybe we should change our behavior. There are, of course, exceptions to this. Some behaviors are more appropriate for one age group than another. When a child imitates a behavior inappropriate for his age group but appropriate for his parents, he should be made aware of why his parents can behave in such a way but he can't. Punishment is often not the best way of teaching the child the difference. Talking to him and telling him why (if it is logical) might be.

A second model characteristic that greatly affects observational learning is the status of the person being observed. In many respects a model's perceived competency and his status are similar, but this is not always the case. For example, it is well known that we tend to pattern some of our behaviors after people of high status even though their competency in the area of the observed behavior might not be as good as ours. People mistake status for competency. Sometimes we imitate a person not because of his competency but because of who he is. An example is that many people can be sucked into an investment deal if their doctor is also investing money. We imitate the doctor because of his status, not because of his competency in investment matters.

Status is another reason why children are very likely to imitate their parents. To the child the parent is a very-high-status person. In fact, many parents have found themselves in embarrassing situations because of how their child perceives their status. One child I know told a group of people that his dad was the boss of the local university. The father simply taught there. But to the child his father was a person of high status and surely must be the boss.

Parents are not the only important models for a child. Other people in the child's environment who are of high status and demonstrated competency are also capable of serving as models for a child. The status of the model may come from several sources. For example, a favorite uncle will have more status than a casual acquaintance. Similarly, some of the child's friends and classmates may be important models for the child. This will be especially true when the friends and classmates are seen to possess desirable qualities. A friend, for example, who is the leader of a gang at school will be a more potent model than someone who is not liked by other children. An example from my own school days will illustrate the power that some age-mate models possess for children. When I was in the seventh grade I was deeply in love with a neighbor girl who was in the ninth grade. But because I was bashful I never told her of my love (except for occasionally sending her unsigned notes). She had a boyfriend whom I hated but whom I began imitating in hopes of gaining the girl's attention. If he wore jeans, I wore jeans. If he walked in a certain way, I walked that way. Maybe, I thought, if I were like my true love's boyfriend, she would notice me. She didn't.

The person a child imitates depends on several characteristics besides status and competency. Sex and age of the model are two very important model characteristics. The relevance of these factors depends upon the behavior being modeled. If the behavior is important for a certain age group, then the most likely model will be someone of that age group. For example, if a young boy is concerned about his clothing, he is more likely to model his dress after someone his age (or slightly older) than after the dress patterns of his parents. Similarly, a male child is more likely to imitate behaviors modeled by another male than he is to imitate a female.

To summarize the characteristics of an effective model for a child, we can say that the most effective model for a child is one who possesses the behaviors that the child desires at the time. Sometimes this model will be the parents. This is especially true for younger children. At other times the most effective model will be one of the child's friends. It depends upon the importance and type of the behavior for the child. If the behavior is important for a child to fit into his age group, then the child is most likely to model a child near his own age. If, on the other hand, the behavior is not specific to the child's age group, he may rely on others who possess the desired behaviors. This brings up an important question: what is it about the model's behavior that makes it desirable? Probably the best answer is that the child sees the behavior as being important for producing rewards. If a child sees someone else being rewarded for a behavior, he is likely to imitate the behavior. Recall the example of the child who told the adult story to his mother's bridge group and the example of how I imitated the boyfriend of my "true love." In both cases the person doing the imitating observed someone being rewarded for some behavior and these rewards were desired. The child who told the story wanted the attention of the adults. I wanted the attention of the girl. It is easy to see why the behaviors were imitated—the observer had seen the imitated behaviors pay off with the desired reward.

Another reason why a child imitates is because he has been previously rewarded for imitating the particular model. For example, many children are rewarded for imitating their parents. Someone might say to the child, "My, you are getting to be a big boy. You do that just like your father." This attention will increase the likelihood that the child will imitate his father again.

Although rewards are important for observational learning, a child, to be influenced by rewards, does not necessarily have to receive the reward. Sometimes his behavior can be changed simply by observing others receive rewards that are desirable to him. In fact, there is some good evidence that these vicarious rewards (rewards given to others, but desired by the child) are responsible for the effect television has on children. When a child watches a television show and observes the hero performing some action which is rewarded, the child is likely to imitate this action. Just think of how many times you've seen your child watch Superman on television and then want you to help make a cape so that he can leap tall buildings and fly faster than a speeding bullet. The influence of television-mediated vicarious rewards is probably desirable when the behaviors the child imitates are socially desirable, but what about when a child is watching cartoons and sees the hero hitting people? These behaviors will also be imitated if the hero is rewarded.

Observer Characteristics.   Are all children equally likely to imitate the behavior of others? It appears not. Just as there were important model characteristics that influenced the likelihood that a child would imitate a model, there are certain child characteristics that affect observational learning. Many of these child characteristics can be thought of as personality factors which have developed through the child's previous interactions with others. Some of the most important child or observer characteristics are dependency, self-esteem, level of competence, and previous experience of imitating someone.

Let's look at some examples of how these characteristics might influence whether or not a child will imitate a model's behavior. Imagine two children. In a certain situation, one has had successful experiences solving problems and the other child has been criticized for his attempts to solve problems. The less successful child, rather than being allowed to work the problem out in his own way was told, "Do it this way.'' Which one is more likely to imitate someone else when he has a problem to solve? Probably the child who has been criticized for his problem-solving attempts. The punishment he received for self-initiated attempts will increase the likelihood of his imitating someone else—especially if the imitated behavior was successful in producing rewards. We might consider this factor—previous successful or unsuccessful attempts to solve problems—as affecting a child's self-confidence. A child who has been successful will be more willing to try things on his own. The less successful child will rely more on someone else to guide his behavior.

A second factor, expertise or competence, will have similar affects. A child who is competent in doing something will be less likely to imitate another person than a child of lower competence. For example, imagine two children working on a reading assignment. One of the children is a skilled reader, the other less skillful. Let's suppose that both of these children have problems reading a new word. Which child will be more likely to try to sound the word out and get the meaning himself, and which child will be more likely to listen to the way someone else uses the word? The child who has reading skills will probably be more successful at handling the problem by himself. He has the necessary competence and will not have to rely on the help of others as much as the child with fewer skills.

The two characteristics described above might give the impression that only children who are inadequate in some way will imitate others. This is obviously not the case. The intention of the above examples was to demonstrate conditions under which a child would be more likely to imitate some. All children, like all adults, have greater or lesser capabilities in certain areas and at certain times. For example, the more competent child in the reading example is probably less competent than his teacher and will observe his teacher and imitate her behavior, but will not imitate a child who has lesser reading skills. The point is, then, that all children imitate. The person imitated and the behaviors the child imitates depends upon the qualities of the model, the rewards available, and the qualities of the child.

Although the characteristics of models and observers described above are important for most cases of observational learning, we can usually encourage imitation regardless of how the child perceives our competencies or his own capabilities by making sure rewards for imitative behavior are very powerful. Rewards will generally override the effects of the other model and observer characteristics.

Another general factor that will increase imitative behavior is to instruct the child to attend because he will later be asked to demonstrate what he has observed. This works well, especially if the child is rewarded when he demonstrates what he has observed.

WHAT CAN A CHILD LEARN BY OBSERVING OTHERS?

We have seen that a child will imitate the actions of other people. Does a child learn more than just the overt, public behaviors that the model performs? Research with children has shown that children learn many things from watching others. The learning that takes place is not restricted to just the way in which a person performs a behavior. A child can also learn attitudes and emotions by observing others.

Performance of Actions

When a child observes and then imitates the way a model moves his hands, walks, sits, and so forth, we can say he is imitating the model's *performance actions*. This is, in fact, the most conspicuous type of imitative learning. We can see a child watch his father and then do the same things his father does. When the child is rewarded for imitating his father's behavior he will be likely to imitate again in the future. Sometimes it is more difficult to observe that a child has also learned attitudes and emotional reactions by observing others.

The specific actions a child learns will depend on several things: how complex the actions are, the ease with which the child can observe the actions, and the emphasis the father places on the actions. If an action is extremely complex, it is less likely that the child will correctly imitate the model. For example, in the book *Flowers for Algernon* (from which the movie *Charly* was made) about a retarded man, one of the men working with Charly tried to show him how to knead dough correctly.[2] His demonstration was far too complex, and Charly failed to imitate all the necessary components of the behavior. This made him feel stupid and it annoyed his friend. Similar failures occur when we try to demonstrate complex behaviors to our children. When a modeled behavior is too complex, the child fails and feels bad. This

---

[2]Keyes, D. *Flowers for Algernon.* New York: Harcourt, Brace and World, 1966.

sometimes causes his parents to be annoyed that the child can't lear, simple (to the parent) behavior. This problem can generally b, eliminated by using the "shaping" procedures described in Chapter 3. Rather than demonstrating the full, complex behavioral sequence, we can demonstrate just part of it. When the child correctly imitates the demonstrated portion we can elaborate the behavioral sequence, making it more complex. This way, the child can learn to imitate a behavior that originally may have been too complex for him to imitate successfully.

A child will also fail to imitate behaviors that are difficult for him to observe. For example, I recall trying to teach a small child the string game cat's cradle. I swiftly wound the string around my fingers and performed hand twists to put the string into the correct designs. When the child tried, he failed. I had been too quick with my demonstrations and he couldn't follow what I was doing. For accurate imitation to occur, the child must be able to discriminate each of the necessary movements. If he misses one or more of the movements, the behavior will not be properly integrated and the child will not have learned the correct behavioral sequence.

Finally, we increase the likelihood that certain behaviors will be imitated by emphasizing those behaviors. For example, assume your child is having difficulty saying the beginning sounds for certain words. He may say the /l/ sound for /y/ to make the word "yes" sound like "les." We can use observational learning procedures to help correct this error in speaking. To increase the effectiveness of our modeled response we might emphasize the part of the word that the child is incorrectly saying. We would say YE-s, YE-llow, and so forth. Our emphasis would be on the part of the word the child says incorrectly. We could emphasize this part of the word by saying it louder and by pausing slightly between the emphasized part and the part of the word the child is saying correctly.

In a natural situation, where you are not intentionally trying to teach a child, he is more or less likely to imitate some, but not all, of your behaviors. He is more likely to imitate those behaviors which you exaggerate and imitate less those behaviors you deemphasize. In other words, the child will not learn to imitate all your behaviors with equal mastery. He will imitate some behaviors better or more correctly than others. The behaviors most likely to be correctly imitated are those that are not complex, are easily discriminated, and receive the most emphasis.

139
a

should point out that a child may acquire a behavior
d, but he may not immediately demonstrate that he
havior. The behavior may not be imitated or per-
d until some later point in time. This brings up an
difference between learning and performance. A child may
learn many things and only perform some of them. Why? Well, it is
probably because of the difference in the conditions that are necessary
for learning to take place and for the performance of the behavior.
For learning to take place it is not absolutely necessary for the child to
be rewarded or to see someone else rewarded for the modeled
behavior. All that is necessary is that the child see some relationship
between the modeled behavior and the stimulus conditions associated
with the behavior. In other words, a child will observe and learn some
task simply by observing someone else perform the task.

A necessary condition for the child to perform what he has learned
is that the child be rewarded for the behavior. This is an important
distinction between learning and performance: for learning to take
place all that is necessary is that two things occur together in time,
while for performance to occur, the child must be rewarded. This was
neatly demonstrated in a research study conducted by Albert Bandura, a psychologist who has extensively studied observational learning. One group of children observed a model engage in a behavior that
was punished. Another group of children observed the model perform
the same behavior, but the model wasn't punished. When the children
were later observed, the children who observed the model being
punished did not imitate the model's behavior. The children who did
not see the model punished did imitate, however. Then, Bandura, to
see if the children who watched the model being punished had learned
the model's behavior, offered the children a reward if they imitated
the punished behavior. They could! They had learned the behavior,
but watching the model being punished discouraged them from performing the behavior.[3] This demonstrated that learning and performance are two different things and occur for different reasons.

This difference between learning and performance has produced
some interesting questions in the minds of parents. A parent will
observe a child engaging in some behavior and wonder where his child
learned it. The actual learning may have taken place some time ago,
but the conditions for the performance may have just occurred.

---

[3]Bandura, A. *Principles of Behavior Modification.* New York: Holt, Rinehart and
Winston, 1969.

Learning Attitudes

When we speak of attitudes, what are we referring to? Don't we mean the way we feel or think about something? For example, if we have a negative attitude toward the amount of violence on television, don't we mean that we dislike television violence and that when we see violent scenes on television we get upset (feeling) and say things to ourselves such as "That is terrible, it shouldn't be allowed on television" (thinking)? We might also express our feelings and thoughts to others. We might say to our neighbor, "Did you see that movie last night on television? I think it was terrible to show those violent scenes." When we are expressing an attitude by feeling, thinking, or talking about something, we are also doing other things—we express our attitudes with our facial expressions, with the way we move our hands, and with our tone of voice. These actions, as well as our talking about our attitudes, are public in the sense that others can see the way we express ourselves. These public or overt expressions of our attitudes can be observed by our children and later imitated when conditions are appropriate.

Let's consider an example of how a child might learn by observation of an attitude toward someone. Let's suppose that you have a very negative attitude toward the way your neighbor treats her children. When you observe her yelling at her children you might frown, shake your head, and say, "That's terrible, the way she treats her children." When this happens, your child might be observing you. At some later point in time, the child might be asked about your neighbor. What do you think he will say? In other words, will he express the attitudes that he has observed you express earlier? He may frown, shake his head, and say the same words you spoke earlier. Your child is imitating your attitude toward your neighbors.

Attitudes that you model for your children (intentionally or unintentionally) will be imitated—especially if the child observes your being rewarded for expressing the attitude. For example, if, when you are talking to a friend you express an attitude and your friend agrees, the child is observing you being socially rewarded for expressing your attitude. This vicarious reward will increase the likelihood that the child will express a similar attitude.

Attitudes, then, are learned in the same way actions are learned. A child's observation of a model being rewarded for exhibiting a particular attitude will probably result in the child expressing the same attitude under similar conditions.

Learning Emotional Behavior

When we react emotionally we provide our children with cues on how to react in similar situations. When we see something that we think is funny, we laugh. If we see something we dislike, we may frown. Because emotions are reactions we learn, a young child will often imitate our emotional expression when he comes in contact with the things that caused our emotional behavior. For example, if you saw a person searching through the pockets of your coat while it was on a hanger in a restaurant, you might react with anger and rush over to the person and say, "What are you doing?" If your child observed this he would be learning what he might think is the appropriate reaction to someone taking something from him without permission. In addition to your rushing forward and saying something to the person, you would also be doing other things. Because of your anger you might be breathing hard, your face might be red, and your hands might be shaking. When you finally talk to your child you might say, "That made me so mad." Look at what you have modeled for the child. First, you've shown him a series of behaviors (approaching and talking to the person), bodily changes associated with emotion (hands shaking, face reddening, and hard breathing), and finally, you've given the child a label for all of these reactions—"I'm mad."

In similar circumstances the child is likely to have similar reactions. He will say things, he will react with certain emotions, and he will tell himself or others that he is mad. Other emotions are similarly learned when children observe others. Once the child has acquired these reactions he will use them in new situations. For example, a child who observes someone hitting his little brother might react in a similar way as his parent did when the coat was being searched. To the child the situational cues are similar enough to evoke similar emotions. In both cases someone was doing something they shouldn't have, and he reacted by being "mad" at the person.

It is obvious that I have oversimplified describing the way a child learns by observing others. For example, when a parent expresses an attitude, a child may or may not imitate the parent's attitude. This will be affected by the child's own experience with the object of the attitude. In the example of the neighbor who mistreats her children, the child may not imitate his mother's statements about the neighbor if he has had positive experiences with the neighbor. His attitude will not only be determined by what he has observed his parents say and do, but also by his own experience with the neighbor and what other people say about the neighbor.

Emotional reactions are not exclusively developed in a child because of what he observes his parents do. Other factors such as those described above will also affect a child's emotional reactions. The other factors may act to modify only slightly the child's imitative behavior, while at other times they will prevent imitation of the modeled behavior. The model, the consequences of the model's behavior, the consequences of the child's imitation, and the effects of other factors such as how other people behave will determine whether the child will imitate a model or if his behavior will differ from the model.

EXAMPLE 9.1

Can a Young Child Teach His Older Brother?

Most of the people whom a child observes and imitates are either his peers or his parents. Sometimes, however, a parent can use a younger child as a model for an older child. This usually happens when the younger child is rewarded for a behavior that the older child should be engaging in, but isn't. Two psychologists, J. J. Johnson and D. J. Thompson, demonstrated how a younger child could be used as an effective model to teach an older child to stop wetting his pants.

A five-year-old boy was referred to the psychologists because of behavior problems and because he was wetting his clothes on the average of eight times a day. The solution to the child's wetting his clothes came as an accident. The mother was beginning to toilet-train the boy's two-and-a-half-year-old brother. The mother had taken the younger child to the toilet and the young child urinated. When the mother praised the young child, the five-year-old asked if it would make the mother proud if he were to go to the toilet like his younger brother. The mother said it certainly would make her proud. The five-year-old walked up to the toilet and urinated! When the delighted mother told the psychologists, they recommended that the mother continue taking the five-year-old to the bathroom and have him observe the younger child being toilet-trained. It worked! The five-year-old almost completely stopped wetting his pants!

From J. J. Johnson and D. J. Thompson, Modeling in the Treatment of Enuresis: A Case Study. *Journal of Behavior Therapy and Experimental Psychiatry*, 1974, Vol. 5, pp. 93–94.

EXERCISE

This exercise is intended as both an awareness exercise and a practical exercise. In order to demonstrate to yourself the powerful influence modeling has on the behavior of others, try to change your behavior and notice the effects it has. Two suggested changes are: (1) increase the number of times you smile at your children (and your spouse); and (2) decrease the loudness of your voice. The latter, voice loudness, is an especially easy change for you to make and might possibly have the greatest effect.

If you do change your rate of smiling or the loudness of your voice, it might be best done in a way that will give you the clearest demonstration of its effect. I would, for example, select certain times of the day to test the effects of your modeled cues. Mealtime would be a good time. During mealtime many families discuss events of the day, often with the discussion centered on what the child has done. If the discussion should include reprimands, there is usually an increase in the loudness of the conversation.

If, however, regardless of what is said, you talk in a soft, quiet voice, you should notice that the others will also begin talking more softly.

This is a very simple demonstration which can show how easily your actions influence the actions of those around you—especially children. If you find you are successful, you might wish to compliment the family (especially those who talked softly) by saying something like: "I sure enjoyed dinner today. The conversation was nice and quiet. I like that." The compliment combined with the cues you provide should produce an interesting change in the loudness of your family's mealtime conversation.

Once you have seen how effective modeling can be, you might wish to work on other, more important changes in your behavior and the behavior of your children.

10
Using Observational Learning Methods To Change Behavior

We say in Chapter 9 that the effects of a child observing a model are rather profound. A model has influence not only on a child's performance of actions, but also on his attitudes and emotions. These effects can be either positive or negative depending upon the way people in the child's environment evaluate the behavior.

Most of the behaviors, attitudes, and emotions that children learn by observing others are learned without the model intentionally teaching the child. But because the methods of observational learning are such powerful teaching devices, they can be used with great success by parents who are intentionally trying to teach their children new and more appropriate ways of behaving. In a sense, just about anything that can be taught using other methods can be taught as effectively using observation learning methods. For example, we can use observational learning methods to teach new behaviors or to reduce inappropriate behaviors. The last case is, of course, typically done using punishment. In the next section we will look at the types of behaviors that can be worked with using observational learning methods.

USING OBSERVATIONAL LEARNING METHODS
WITH DIFFERENT TYPES OF BEHAVIORS

Since teaching of new behaviors using observational learning procedures has been described earlier, I will only briefly summarize the important considerations of how a parent can teach his child new behaviors. The first requirement is that the model be someone who is of high status or possesses the revelant skills. Parents are especially powerful models because their children feel the parent is very knowledgeable. Secondly, the task to be taught to the child should be one that is relevant to his life. A child will imitate those behaviors that he feels are important for producing rewards more readily than those which do not seem to have a positive payoff. Third, the cues (behaviors) modeled for the child must not be too complex and must be easily discriminated, and the most important cues should be emphasized. Fourth, observational learning can be facilitated by instructing the child to pay attention to the model's behavior. Finally, either the model should be observed being rewarded for the demonstrated behavior or the child should be rewarded for imitating the modeled behavior.

Using these principles, a parent can effectively teach a child many new behaviors. The same principles are also important for the other effects of observational learning, but they are presented here rather than repeated again in other sections.

Facilitating Existing Behaviors

From what you have read about observational learning, how would you go about teaching your child to play cooperatively more often with his sister? Let's suppose that the child already cooperates a certain amount, but usually only when he benefits from the cooperative play. For example, he is willing to cooperate when he needs someone to play one of his favorite games, but not when his sister wants to play one of her games. How would you teach the child to play cooperatively with his sister when she chooses the game? To begin, you might consider what the necessary ingredients are for successful observational learning to occur. First, we need a model. Who might be a good model? Well, you might. Or an older brother or sister. You might even consider having one of his friends over and ask him to play with the sister. Any of these models might be effective. There might be others such as grandparents, uncles, and aunts who might be very good models. The point is that it shouldn't be difficult to find an effective model who your child will imitate.

Next, we need to think of a reward that will be effective for encouraging the child to play with his sister. You could give the reward to the model and indicate that the reward is available to all who play the game. Let's suppose that an effective reward for the child might be going for a ride in the car. With the choice of the model and the reward we have the basic ingredients for observational learning to occur. How do we put them together?

Let's assume that you have chosen the child's older brother as the model. You might wish to explain to him what you are doing and why, although this is not absolutely necessary. Next, find some way of encouraging the boy's sister to suggest a game that requires cooperation. When the girl suggests the game, you might act delighted and say, "What a good idea. I think that will be fun." The model should also express excitement about playing. Now, you might say, "When we've finished playing and cooperating, let's go for a ride in the car." If the excitement of playing the game and the desire for the reward are not effective for getting the child to play with his sister, you might have to do more. For example, you might say to the boy, "Would you like to play the game and then go for a ride?" Several prompts like this and the model's expressions of joy should be adequate to capture the child into playing. If he does imitate the model and begin playing with his sister, it is important that he be immediately rewarded. You could do this by saying how much you enjoy seeing your children playing together. Then remind them of the car ride.

One situation like this will probably be inadequate to increase the boy's cooperative play with his sister. You should plan on repeating similar situations several times and if possible using different models each time. The more people engaging in the behavior, the more likely it is that your child will imitate the models.

From this example, we can see that the procedures for increasing the number of times a child engages in a given behavior are not that different from teaching the child a new behavior. When we are trying to increase a behavior the problem is not *how to teach* the behavior, but *how to increase* the behavior. The behavior might not be occurring as frequently as we would like because the rewards for the behavior are not powerful enough or because the child has been punished for similar behaviors in the past. In either case, the basic method of increasing the behavior is to increase the potency of rewards for the behavior. You could reward the child more frequently than before or make the rewards more desirable.

A second reason a child might not engage in a behavior as frequently as we would like is that the range of stimuli influencing his behavior is too narrow. This means that the child has only learned to do the behavior in some settings but not in others. In this case, our problem is to increase the number of stimuli controlling the child's behavior. Take a child, for example, who plays happily at home and at the homes of his grandparents and his best friends, but refuses to play at the homes of other children. The child may also not play when you are visiting friends. At the home of your friends he may just sit or want to be by you. The task there is to increase the range of situations where the child will play. How can we go about this task? Let's say for purposes of illustration that you want to get your child to play at the neighbor's when you are visiting. The neighbor has a child a year or so younger than your child, but when you have visited your neighbor in the past your child wouldn't play with the neighbor child. How could you encourage him to play? Using the ideas of observational learning you might arrange to have your neighbor invite the mother of a friend of your child to visit and bring her child. If this older child can be encouraged to play at the neighbor's, he might be an effective model for your child. If your child's friend does begin to play with the neighbor's child, it is important that the children who are playing be rewarded. You might also point out to your child how much fun the other children are having and how neat the neighbor boy's toys are. This will often be adequate to get your child to play—at least a little bit. If he does, reward him.

For observational teaching to be most effective in this example and in the example of encouraging the child to play with his sister, you should be careful to not expect too much from the child. If he plays for a few minutes the first time, be satisfied. After he has played for a brief period of time take him home or change the routine. You want to make sure that you end the play on a positive note. Don't let the child remain in the situation until it becomes unpleasant. If you do, you will have defeated the purpose of what you are trying to teach the child.

Eliminating Inappropriate Behaviors

We have seen that rewarding a model in the child's presence has motivating effects for the child. The child, after observing a model engage in some behavior that is rewarded, will often imitate the model's behavior. We called this a *vicarious reward effect*. Vicarious rewards provide an additional dimension to the power of rewards. Not only do the rewards that a child receives affect his behavior, but rewards given to others can also increase the likelihood that the child will engage in a given behavior. Does punishment have similar effects? Will punishment given to a model decrease the likelihood that the child will engage in the modeled behavior? Yes. The research evidence on this is quite clear: punishment, to be effective for reducing the likelihood of a child's behavior, does not have to be delivered to the child. Sometimes it is enough to have the child observe a model being punished for a behavior in order to effectively decrease the child's behavior.

Many parents have observed this with their own children. A parent might walk into a room where his child and several other children are misbehaving and punish her child for the misbehavior. The punishment her child receives stops all of the children from engaging in the inappropriate behavior. Why does this work? Possibly the vicarious effects of punishment and rewards are due to the child being able to empathize with the person being punished or rewarded. In other words, because the child has had similar experiences in the past, he can understand and "feel" how the other person reacts to the punishment or rewards. He might also anticipate similar punishment if he engages in the punished behavior.

Let's look at how the vicarious effects of punishment might work for effectively reducing your child's inappropriate behavior. Let's imagine that you have a child who has recently begun sneaking cigarettes and smoking them. You consider smoking to be undesirable and would like to encourage your child not to smoke. How might you use observational learning procedures to accomplish this? For some children, seeing a film or demonstration of someone with a lung disease can be very effective. Some films show people who are unable to engage in normal activities because their lungs are in such bad shape. Or the film might show a person who has a breathing hole in his throat because he has had cancer of the throat. Watching these incapacitated people often serves as vicarious punishment to decrease a child's smoking.

Another tactic that might work with young children is for you or one of your child's favorite relatives who doesn't smoke to model smoking in front of the child and complain about the effects. For example, you could invite the favored relative to your house and tell him, in front of your child, that your child is thinking of starting smoking. The relative might then say, "I've been thinking I also might start smoking. Let me have a cigarette." The relative could then light the cigarette and complain about the taste and how it makes him feel. If the relative is important to the child, the vicarious punishment of smoking might decrease the child's desire to smoke.

An advantage of the use of vicarious punishment is that the child doesn't have to directly experience the negative effects of punishment. This is especially valuable when some of the punishments arranged by society are very severe. It would probably be better, for example, to have your child observe the punishment someone receives for being caught for shoplifting than to be sent to a juvenile home for the same offense.

One problem with the vicarious punishment procedure is that if a child observes a model engage in an inappropriate behavior and the model is *not punished,* the effect on the observing child is similar to the model being rewarded for the behavior. The child will be more likely to imitate the model. The concern this finding should produce for parents is that we should not "let another child off" with performing a behavior if our child is observing. Our child may imitate the other child. We may have to solve this by telling our child something like "If I were that boy's parent, I would spank him."

Reinstating Behaviors

Sometimes children stop engaging in a behavior that they are perfectly capable of performing. For example, a young child I know used to love to play with dogs. All of a sudden he would not go near a dog. If his parents tried to lead him to a dog, the child would act frightened. Although the parents were uncertain why the child began acting this way, they were convinced that the child must have had a bad experience with dogs. Because many of their friends had dogs they were concerned that their child might become upset when they went visiting. They decided to try an observational learning approach to reinstate their child's enjoyment of dogs. The procedure they used was similar to the systematic desensitization procedure described in Chapter 8. One day they went to visit a friend who owned a small, very quiet dog. Prior to the visit, they had called the friend and told them that they would like to use their dog to help the child get over his fear of dogs. The friends took the dog out on to the back lawn at the opposite end of the yard. The father did several things to keep the child relaxed; he played with him, gave him ice cream, and held him on his lap. Over a period of about an hour, the father moved the child progressively closer to the dog. This was done without mentioning the dog to the child or otherwise bringing the dog to the child's attention. When they were finally fairly close to the dog, the father went over and began petting the dog. In a few minutes the child approached the dog, but stood behind his father. Finally, the child cautiously petted the dog. This slow and easy approach to reducing the child's fear and increasing the child's contact with the dog continued for several visits. At the end of three visits, the child seemed to have no fear of the dog and readily approached the dog and played with him. He later played with other dogs. The child learned not to fear the dog and to play with dogs by observing his father approach the dog and not suffer from the experience. This indicates that observational learning procedures have value for teaching children many different aspects of behavior.

Observational learning can be used to teach a child new behaviors; to increase the frequency of behaviors that the child already does, but not often enough; to decrease inappropriate behaviors without having to punish the child; and to reinstate behaviors that the child once engaged in but has, for some reason, discontinued. Observational learning is a powerful and convenient method for teaching children.

OBSERVATIONAL LEARNING OF RULES
RATHER THAN OF SPECIFIC BEHAVIORS

Sometimes when we are trying to teach a child how to behave appropriately, we want to do more than just teach him to perform a specific behavior in a specific place. What we might want is for the child to use the behavior, or similar behaviors, in a wide variety of situations. For example, a parent who is teaching his child to say "please" and "thank you" at the dinner table would probably want his child to use "please" and "thank you" in other settings. The parent might also want the child to use other polite words when they are appropriate. This is quite a different situation than when we teach specific behaviors. When we teach specific behaviors, we can't expect that they will automatically occur in other settings. Nor can we expect that teaching a child a specific behavior will cause the child to use other, similar behaviors more frequently. If the parent wants the child to be more general in his use of certain behaviors, then it is necessary that the parent intentionally teach the more general use of the behaviors. This can be done by teaching the child rules rather than specific behaviors. Observational learning procedures can be very helpful for teaching such rule-governed behavior.

Let's use an example to illustrate the way in which rule-governed behavior can be taught to a child and how teaching rule-governed behavior differs from teaching specific behaviors. Consider how a parent might teach his child to act politely. The parent is interested not only in teaching his child to say "please" and "thank you" at the dinner table, but also in teaching the child to use these terms in other situations and to use other polite terms and behaviors in appropriate situations. How could the parent do this? Using the concepts of observational learning, the parent might instruct his child in a basic rule such as "When people do nice things for you, it is proper that you should let them know that you appreciate what they have done." The parent may elaborate this rule to include "When you want something from someone, you should ask them politely." Once the rule has been told to the child, the parent should try to model the appropriate behaviors. When he provides an example of the behavior or when the child engages in an example of the rules, it should be pointed out. For example, let's suppose the child had just completed playing with a friend and as the friend was about to leave the child's house, the child said, "Thanks for coming over, Joe. It was a lot of fun." When this happened the parent should say something like, "Tom, that was very nice to thank Joe for coming over. That was a good example of the politeness rule that we were talking about last night. It was fun to play with Joe and you thanked him. I like that."

When a parent teaches a child a rule rather than a specific behavior, the child becomes more capable of transferring the behavior to new situations. This occurs because the child has not learned just behaviors, but has developed a concept where he is able to classify things together and to react to these things in a similar manner.

Teaching Rule-Governed Behavior

In many situations, it is obvious that rule-governed behavior is more desirable than when a child has just learned specific behaviors for specific situations. What can a parent do to increase the likelihood that his child will be able to learn basic rules which govern his behavior? There are three basic aids a parent can use in teaching rule-governed behavior: varying the irrelevant information, but keeping the rule constant; using rule-relevant instructions; and having a variety of people model the behavior from which the rule is abstracted. We will discuss each of these in turn.

Keeping the Rule Constant. One way of increasing the likelihood that a child will be able to abstract out the rule you wish him to learn is to model a variety of behaviors where the rule is important to all of the behaviors, but the other information differs. For example, let's say that you want to teach your child how to understand the meaning of numbers. You could do this by saying, ''I want to show you how to use different numbers. Here we have one boat. How many? One? That's right! Now here are two boats. How many? Two—that's good.'' If you repeat this with many items, you are varying the irrelevant material (the objects), but keeping constant the rule: say one when there is only one object, but two when you have two items.

Notice that in the example, two of the important ingredients for good teaching are present: you are providing cues by saying the number, and you are rewarding the child for correct answers to your question ''How many?'' In this situation the child is very likely to be able to abstract the number rule and use it when you present him with new objects without modeling the correct response. If the child does get the answer to ''how many'' correct without your modeling the answer, you have a good indication that he has learned the difference between one and two.

The basic idea of varying the examples and holding the rule constant can be used in a large variety of situations. Let's look at another example where what we want to teach the child is a more complex behavior. Let's consider an example of how a parent I know taught her retarded child how to greet people. The mother was concerned because the child would greet all people by running up and kissing and hugging them. The mother was afraid this might create two kinds of problems: some people might be annoyed by the child's greeting, and secondly, the girl was a reasonably attractive teenager who might cause some trouble for herself with her overfriendly greeting.

After considering the type of people that the girl would be likely to greet, the mother formulated a rule she wanted to teach the girl: you can greet relatives with a hug and kiss, neighbors and friends are to be greeted by shaking hands, and strangers are to be greeted by saying hello. To teach this rule, the mother invited a number of people to visit the girl and, before they arrived, the mother explained the rule to them and to the girl. When the visitors arrived, the mother modeled the correct greeting behavior. If the girl correctly imitated the mother, the child was socially rewarded. After greeting just a few people in each category, the girl seemed to have grasped the rule. She greeted people according to the rule her mother had formulated.

Again, with this example, we see the basic characteristics of teaching rule-governed behavior: vary the irrelevant information, but keep the important component (rule) constant.

Using Rule-Relevant Instructions. If, prior to modeling the behaviors we want the child to imitate, we tell the child what rule we want him to learn, we can sometimes speed up the acquisition of rule-governed behavior. Instructing the child as to the rule is not always helpful, however. The instructions, to be of value, must be informative and contain little if any irrelevant information. If the instructions are not salient to the task, they can actually interfere with the learning. Let's consider two examples of instructions combined with modeling. In the first example I have made the instructions informative and to the point. In the second example the rules are less salient.

Example 1. A parent wants to teach her child to respond quickly to parental requests. When the parent asked the child to do something such as get his clothes on, the child would say, "OK, in a minute," and then go on with what he was doing. To teach the child to react more rapidly the mother rewarded the child's sister for quickly complying with requests. The parent was hoping the "dawdling" child would imitate his sister. To assist the child in learning the mother said to the child, "When I ask you to do something and you do it very quickly, I will give you a mark on your chart." This rule was general enough to cover most of the types of responses to parent requests to be useful for helping the child learn the rule of complying with requests. Secondly, the rule told the child that the behavior was to be completed quickly. It might have been better to tell the child that he should comply within a specific time period, but this time might not be appropriate for all requests, so the parent simply stressed quick compliance. Finally, the instructions told the child the payoff for quick compliance to the parents' requests: a mark on his chart. These instructions were to the point and did not contain irrelevant information that might confuse the child. Compare the instructions in this example with those in the next.

Example 2.   Let's use the same situation, but have the parent give the child different instructions. In this case the parent told the child, "I want you to start obeying me when I ask you to do things. I want you to hurry and do what I ask. It annoys me when you are slow. I don't think it is nice when you goof around when your dad and I ask you to do things. I'll tell you what, if you do decide to be better about doing the things we ask, we'll start giving you a mark on your chart if we think you've been good."

Look at how the instructions in the second example differed from the first. These instructions, although they contain the information from the first set of instructions, include comments about the child's worth, they are preachy and leave vague the conditions under which the child will receive a reward. These instructions are probably not very likely to help the child understand what the parents want to teach him and may interfere with the learning.

What should be contained in instructions that are to help a child learn a rule which will help him behave appropriately in a variety of situations? The rule should contain a specific statement of the desired behavior, the conditions under which the behavior should occur, and the payoff for the behavior. Any additional information can be superfluous and may not aid in teaching the child.

Using Several Models.   Sometimes a rule can be made more relevant if the child sees several people engaging in the appropriate behavior. For example, if you were trying to teach a child to share with others, you might be more effective if you were to point out instances where you see others sharing. The more cases that the child observed, the more likely he would be to imitate the sharing behaviors of others. In addition, the child would have had an opportunity to observe sharing in a variety of different situations.

It is possible that much of a child's natural learning of rules occurs because he has an opportunity to observe and imitate many different models. If this is true, then we should be able to put this information to work and intentionally increase the range of the child's appropriate behaviors. For example, let's consider an example we discussed earlier where we showed how a father was able to reduce his child's fear of dogs by using observational learning procedures. The father might have increased the power of his teaching if he had had several people approach and play with the dog. When the father approached the dog, this might have meant little to the child because the child might have felt that his father was especially brave. If several others had approached the dog, the fear of dogs might have been lessened because the child might have seen that others whom he considered less brave than he were able to approach the dog.

In summary, the basic strategy for using observational learning procedures to teach rule-governed behavior is to present clear information where the basic rule is obvious, but the information that is irrelevant to the rule must be either kept at a minimum or allowed to vary. Rule learning is especially powerful because of the fact that the child is able to use similar behaviors in a variety of situations without having to understand the differences in each situation. In other words, the child has formed a concept where he sees things as being related and the behaviors in each situation as being governed by the same rules.

The importance of a good model for teaching a child should not be underestimated. A child is constantly learning from others, and he will use those models that are most effective in producing rewards. In our social system behaviors that are considered appropriate are the ones that should receive the most rewards. By modeling socially appropriate behaviors we will be encouraging our child to imitate our behavior so as to increase the number of social rewards he receives. When the child imitates our behavior he will then receive these rewards, which will be effective in maintaining the behaviors he originally learned by imitating good models.

In the next chapter, we will look at how modeling procedures can be combined with the child's imagination or thinking processes. The advantage of using the child's imagination is that many behaviors you might wish to teach your child are, for one reason or another, difficult to model.

EXERCISE

Sometimes when parents wish to teach their children more appropriate ways of behaving they try to change everything at once. This usually produces frustration for both parents and children. A better way to implement a behavior change program would be to select one or two behaviors to begin with. This way you are more likely to be successful and not frustrate your children.

Which behavior should you begin with? A rule of thumb would be to select a behavior to teach that has the following properties:

1. The inappropriate behavior is of concern to the child or to his parents. The appropriate behavior to be taught will improve the child's relationship with his parents or with others.

2. The parents are capable of teaching the behavior. A behavior that takes place in the school, say, is not as easy for the parents to work on and should be delayed until you have more experience with some of the ideas you will use.

3. The new behavior will be appropriate to a variety of situations. In other words, teach a new behavior where a general rule can be established that will help the child be successful in a variety of situations.

4. The new behavior can be modeled for the child. For most children *seeing* examples as well as *hearing* what he should do makes it easier to learn the behavior.

Using the above guidelines, try to teach your child or children a new behavior. Two common complaints I often hear are "My children don't pick up after themselves" and "My children won't do what I ask them to do." If your child or children are like this, you might consider working on these problems. Let's use noncompliance as an example of a behavior that you wish to work on and see how it might be done.

First, what do you wish to teach? How about this: "I want my child to respond to my requests within fifteen seconds unless she is engaged in another important activity." This is a fairly good description of what we wish to teach.

Second, we should instruct the child as to what we want. The instructions should be positive, stating what is desired and the payoff. For example, you might say: "Susan, I want to teach you to do things when I ask you to do them. Beginning today if you will do what I ask as quickly as possible, I'll let you stay up an hour later at night. If you are busy with something important, tell me what you are doing then say, 'I'll do it as soon as I'm finished.' If you do what I've asked after you've finished, I'll still let you stay up."

Third, you should model examples of what you want. You might say, for example: "Let me show you what I mean. You pretend you are me and I'll be you. I want you to ask me to come to dinner." When the child requests the behavior, you comply immediately and pleasantly or say, for example, "I'm washing my hands, I'll be in as soon as I'm through."

The second way to model the behavior is to comply with your child's requests in the same way you are asking her to. It's hard to ask a child to do something we are unwilling to do. By complying with the child's requests you are giving her examples of the "compliance" rule. This will help her to learn that the behavior is appropriate in a variety of situations.

Finally, when examples of appropriate behavior occur, they should be socially rewarded as well as rewarded later as stated in the instructions.

11

Using the Child's Imagination

Much of a child's world is imaginative. Children play by themselves, yet talk as if others were around; they create situations that bear little or no resemblence to physical reality. The imaginative life exists for several purposes. It is a source of fun for the child and it is a source of experimentation. In a child's imagination he can "try out" new behaviors or he can rehearse behaviors that he is soon to engage in. This section will describe some of the ways in which parents can use a child's imagination to help their children develop new and better ways of interacting with the world.

It is surprising how little is known about how a child uses his imagination. The volumes of work that have been published have only broken the surface of what goes on in a "child's head." As this knowledge grows we are bound to find that the child's imagination will provide parents with even more raw material from which to help develop the capabilities and behaviors of their children.

When faced with a difficult problem, some children either quickly give up or guess at the correct answer. Often this answer is selected at random and has no relationship to the real answer. This inability of some children to focus on a problem and work it through to its correct solution has attracted the attention of several psychologists. These psychologists found that impulsive children spend less time "thinking" the problem through and make random guesses at correct answers. Good problem solvers, on the other hand, talk to themselves while solving problems. They use talk to direct their problem-solving behavior. For example, a child who is good at solving problems might approach a problem of classifying a group of toys into four groups in the following way:

Child: (*Talking aloud or to himself*) I'm supposed to put these things together in their right groups. Let's see, some are red and some are blue. I'll put the blue ones here and the red ones here. Wait a minute! Some of the blue ones are animals and some of the red ones are animals. I'll put the blue animals here and the red animals here. Good, I've done that. What about the others? They're all cars. Oh, I'll put the red cars into this pile and the blue cars into this pile. Is that right? It looks good.

Notice that the child, whom we might call a reflective child, talked to himself in specific ways. He reflected on the problem and talked to himself in ways that would bring him closer to solving the problem. Initially he established the problem: he had to put things into correct groups. Then he started looking for features that made the objects different. At first he noticed the color and began classifying the objects on that basis. While doing this, he noticed that the objects were animals or cars. That is, he questioned his choices. So, he put all the cars of one color together and all the animals of the same color together. Then he began working on the other color. Notice that the child rewarded himself for making a good choice.

How does a child learn problem-solving behavior? One way is by watching his parents or other capable problem solvers at work. Your child might listen to you say, while teaching him to tie his shoelaces, "OK, John, what do we do first? Let's pull the laces tight. That's right. Now, put one lace over the other. What next? That's right—put one lace up through the other. . . ." Many parents will teach their child through a combination of modeled cues and by instructing their child. But while the parent is instructing the child he is also asking questions about what should be done next. This teaches the child to question what he is doing and how best to do it. The parent is also providing rewards (to himself and to the child) for correct behaviors. The rewards, as we know, increase the likelihood that the child will repeat the behavior. As the child is faced with new problems he is likely to imitate the problem-solving approach that he observed his parents use. In fact, the child may use many of the specific questions the parent asked: What do we do first? What do we do next? and so forth.

TEACHING CHILDREN TO TALK TO THEMSELVES

D.H. Meichenbaum, a Canadian psychologist, wondered if children who were impulsive and had difficulty staying with a task could be taught to be more reflective. He found they could: impulsive children can be taught to give themselves instructions that make them much more efficient at solving problems.[1]

How did Meichenbaum go about teaching the children? Several research studies indicated to Dr. Meichenbaum that young children are not capable of using their own language to regulate their behavior, but their behavior can be regulated by someone else talking. Later children can talk aloud and respond to their own talking. It is only after a child has learned to talk aloud to himself that he can learn to talk privately to himself (think) and use his private conversation to control his behavior. In other words, at first a child is dependent upon external sources of information to control his behavior, later he can provide the necessary cues by talking aloud to himself. And at some later time he can use his thinking or imagination to control his actions.

Using this developmental approach to how a child learns to use his language to control his behavior, Meichenbaum set out to teach behavior. At first, he had children observe a model solve a problem while the model talked to himself. Then he had the children imitate the model and talk aloud about how to handle the problem. Later the children were encouraged to whisper or talk to themselves while solving a problem.

When the children were tested following training, they were far less impulsive and much more likely to solve a problem correctly. The children had learned to control their own behavior by talking to themselves!

[1]Meichenbaum, D.H. and Goodman, J. Training Impulsive Children to Talk to Themselves: A Means of Developing Self-Control. *Child Development,* 1969, Vol. 40, pp. 785–797.

Can a parent use Dr. Meichenbaum's teaching strategy with their own children? Let's consider a common problem that might be improved by teaching a child to talk to himself. If a child is asked to make his bed he will often try in a haphazard way and see that the results are not nearly as good as when his mother makes the bed. Sometimes the child will get frustrated and say, "I can't do it." If this happens, the mother might say, "Watch me. I'll show you how." As she begins to make the bed she could say, "OK, what do I do first? Let's see, I'll take the pillows off the bed. That will make it easier to pull the blankets up. Now, I'll pull back the blankets and straighten the sheets. How does that look? Good? Yes, that's fine." The parent can continue to describe each of the necessary parts of making the bed and occasionally question if it is correct.

When the parent has completed making the bed she might mess it up and have the child make it. The parent could describe each sequence to the child using a conversational manner where the child is asked if each step is correct. Later, the parent can have the child make the bed and say aloud each step that he is to perform. If the child is rewarded for using self-instruction and for correctly completing the task, he is likely to use self-instructions the next time he has to make the bed.

Teaching a child to use self-instructions can sometimes be greatly facilitated if the parent encourages the child to use his imagination. Let's consider how a child might be encouraged to use imaginative self-instruction to improve his handwriting. One of the child's problems with writing is that he hurries and his letters are poorly formed and run off the lines. His parent might tell him, "Practice making your letters slower. Tell yourself to be like a turtle. Say to yourself, 'I will go no faster than a slow turtle.'" The addition of the imaginative component might make the task of self-instruction more fun and also more concrete. It might have been that just telling the child to go slow was not enough. He might have watched you write the letters and used your speed as a comparison. The comparison of a turtle might emphasize slowness more effectively.

As with the teaching strategies we've discussed earlier, we shouldn't expect the child to immediately improve his performance when he begins self-instructing while performing a task. It is a new way of behaving, and you might have to practice it with him several times before it "sinks in." To encourage the child's use of self-instructions, we should try to have the child self-instruct on simple tasks before moving to more complex ones. In fact, one good way to teach a child to self-instruct would be to start on a task that he already performs quite well. This will give him practice working on something he knows reasonably well, and he might be able to see the advantage of self-instructions more readily.

When a child is learning how to talk to himself you should try to encourage him to use his own questions and descriptions of the tasks rather than simply parroting what you say. If a child simply repeats what you say, you are unsure whether he is just saying the words and using some other method of controlling his own behavior. But if he uses his own descriptions, we can see how closely they correspond to his performance. This will give us a good idea of how carefully he is using self-generated instructions to control his behavior.

One way of encouraging your child to use task-relevant instructions is to have him teach a younger child how to perform the task. This will "force" the child to use task descriptions that will be helpful to the younger child. If your child does use good instructions, point out how self-instructions might help with some of his own problems.

The idea of talking to oneself as a positive behavior is very different from considering it as a sign of insanity. If self-talk is devoted to solving problems, it is probably a good sign. Most of us, as adults, talk to ourselves, but we do it so no one can hear us—we call it thinking. But notice when you are alone and you are working on a difficult problem. You'll probably find that you talk aloud to yourself. If it helps you solve your problem, go ahead and talk to yourself.

Children are more likely to talk to themselves than are adults because children are less proficient at talking privately to themselves in the way we call thinking. This comes as the child gets older. You might want to take advantage of the child's talking aloud to himself when he is solving a problem to encourage good problem-solving attack skills such as those mentioned above.

A child not only learns to think about how to solve problems more effectively, he can also learn to use his imagination to create other experiences that will help him interact with others more effectively. We adults, for example, will often think about how we are going to act when we meet someone for the first time. Or we may rehearse in our minds what we are going to say to someone when we are angry. When we do this type of thinking or imagining we generally do more than "think" about the words we will use. We imagine ourselves in the situation. In our mind's eye we can visualize how the other person will look, his reactions to what we say, and how we will feel.

This ability of people to imagine events can be used very effectively to teach people new ways of behaving. For example, Dr. Cautela, a well-known psychotherapist, has been treating people who have inappropriate fears by having them imagine themselves in a fear-provoking situation and eventually mastering their fear. Often, if the content of their imagination has been carefully directed by a skilled therapist, the person will be free of the fear in real life. It appears that what the person learned when imagining himself in the fear situation can transfer to real life. Cautela called this treatment procedure *covert modeling*: covert because it takes place in the person's mind, and modeling because the person in real life imitates what his imagined model did.[2]

The advantages of covert modeling are: (1) as in regular modeling, a person learns by observing others and does not have to go through the learning experience himself; (2) the model can be an imagined model, which increases the range of behaviors that can be modeled; and (3) the modeled behaviors can be made to correspond exactly to the person's problems. A final advantage is that covert modeling is a very successful treatment procedure.

When covert modeling procedures are used with children they are changed somewhat to accommodate the child's imaginal capabilities. Sometimes children have a difficult time clearly imagining themselves in a situation—especially if the situation causes the child to be frightened. One way that psychologists have helped increase a child's imagination and attention to problem areas is to tell the child a story that includes the child's problem.

USING STORIES TO TEACH CHILDREN

To illustrate how stories can be used to teach children, let's consider a case example reported by Drs. Lazarus and Abramovitz. They were working with a young girl who wet the bed at night and who was afraid of going to school.[3] To reduce the child's fear of school, they told her stories involving "Noddy," a fictional character. Noddy was placed into school situations that were progressively more challenging.

[2]Cautela, J.R. Covert Modeling. Paper Presented to the Association for the Advance of Behavior Therapy, Washington, D.C., 1971.

[3]Lazarus, A.A. and Abramovitz, A. The Use of "Emotive Imagery" in the Treatment of Children's Phobias. *Journal of Mental Science,* 1962, Vol. 108, pp. 191-195.

The child could help Noddy by being reassuring or setting a good example. Using this teaching method, only four sessions were required to effectively reduce the girl's fear of school. In addition, as often happens when one problem behavior is eliminated, the girl discontinued bed wetting within a few months without further therapeutic attention.

This example demonstrates that stories can be a very effective method for changing a child's behavior. The story presents a situation that the child can identify as being similar to his own. This helps the child identify with the character in the story who is able to solve the problem.

The use of stories as a teaching method actually has a very long history. In ancient times, stories were the main way in which the rules of a society were passed on from generation to generation. This is still true in some groups of people, such as the Eskimos of North America. Our knowledge of how children learn should make stories even more effective.

Features of a Good Teaching Story

A good teaching story should do several things: it should capture the child's attention, it should center around the child's problem, it should provide a convenient way of solving the problem, and it should provide rewards to the story character who has solved the problem. Let's look at a story and see how these elements are interwoven into the story. The story we will consider was told to a five-year-old boy, Tom, who had recently developed a fear of dogs. His parents had previously tried talking to Tom about his fears, but with little success. As a result, the father told Tom this story:

> Once upon a time a boy named Tom went for a walk through the woods with his father. After they had walked a little way, they heard a lot of people talking. The people sounded very upset. Tom and his father went to see what was the matter. When they got to where the people were, Tom said, "What is the matter?"
> A lady who was crying said that her dog had crawled into a cave and was stuck. Some of the people had tried to crawl in and help get the dog loose, but they were too big. They couldn't reach the dog.
> Tom and his father got down on their knees and looked into the cave. They couldn't see the dog because it was very dark in the cave. Then Tom remembered that he had a flashlight in his backpack. He shined the light into the cave where he saw the little dog. The dog's leg was

caught between two rocks. The dog looked at Tom with big brown eyes and began to wag his tail. Tom remembered that someone told him dogs smile by wagging their tails.

Just as Tom was standing up the lady said to Tom, "Do you think you could crawl into the cave and save my dog?"

At first Tom was a little frightened. Sometimes dogs made him a little afraid. Then he looked at the lady who was very sad because her dog was stuck in the cave. Tom said, "I'll try to get your dog loose." The lady was so happy she gave Tom a hug and said, "You're so brave."

Tom's father tied a rope around Tom's waist so he could pull Tom out of the cave if Tom had problems, and Tom began crawling into the cave. At first he was a little nervous, but when he saw the dog in the light of his flashlight, the dog looked very friendly so Tom was no longer afraid. He crawled and crawled to where the dog was. After he petted the dog's head to make the dog feel less nervous, he reached over and pulled the dog's leg free from the rocks.

"Okay, Dad," Tom called as he held the dog tightly in his arms so the dog wouldn't get stuck again. "I've got the dog. Pull us out."

Tom's father and one of the other men pulled on the rope, and Tom and the dog came out of the cave. When Tom stood up he was covered with dust, but the dog was so happy it licked Tom's hand. Tom kneeled down and patted the dog and said, "You're OK now, boy. I got you free."

All of the people cheered Tom and told him what a brave boy he was. A man even took Tom's picture and the next day the picture was in the newspaper with a story of how Tom had bravely saved the dog.

What are the important features of this story? One of the most important was that the father used "Tom" as the hero of the story. This allowed the child to identify closely with the hero of the story. The boy in the story was named Tom, and he was also afraid of dogs.

A second important feature of the story was that the story was designed to reduce the child's fear in the situation. The child's fear was reduced by making the dog appear small and friendly. If it had been a big dog which acted mean, it might have been more difficult to reduce the child's fear. Recall from Chapter 8, when we were discussing systematic desensitization, I mentioned that one way to help reduce a child's fear is to begin by describing things that produce little fear. As the child is able to handle his fear to these things we can make the stimuli more fear-producing. The child, because of his experience of handling a little fear, will be able to better handle the more intense fear stimuli.

Another feature of the story that served to reduce the child's fear was the presence of his father. Sometimes we can effectively reduce a child's fear if he can imagine being with someone who makes him feel safe. Lazarus, whom we talked about earlier, described a case where he reduced a child's fear of going to a dentist by having the child imagine that Batman and Robin accompanied him to the dentist.[4]

A third important feature of the story was that the child learned to cope with his fear. At first the child was afraid of the dog, but because he wanted to help the lady he overcame his fear. His fear was further reduced when he saw the dog was friendly. This is important. Research evidence has shown that training procedures which use models who are at first afraid but progressively cope with their fear are more effective than those where the model is totally fearless. The importance of a coping model might be because a model who copes with his fear is similar to the fearful child. This makes identification easier. Another factor influencing the importance of a coping model is that while the model is coping, the person telling the story has more opportunity to describe the behaviors necessary for coping with the fear. This is analogous to "shaping." Recall from Chapter 7 that I showed that learning occurs more rapidly if the parent rewards the child for closer and closer approximations to the goal behavior. If the parent waited until the child engaged in the goal behavior, it might never occur, and the child would not have an opportunity to be rewarded. The same might be true when using stories.

The fourth important feature of the story which deserves comment is that the story was placed into a framework that was interesting to the child and was likely to keep his attention. If the story had not been interesting, the child would not have paid attention to the way the model coped with his fear. The inattentive child would have learned little. To make a story effective it is necessary that the child attend to the important details. One way of making the details conspicuous is to make the story interesting. Another is to make the story resemble experiences in the child's own life.

Finally, the importance of rewards should again be noted. In the story the child was socially praised for his brave behavior of saving the dog. The rewards in the story are vicarious, but as we saw in the chapter on observational learning, vicarious rewards are sometimes as effective as rewards given directly to the child.

[4]Lazarus, A.A. and Abramovitz, A. The Use of "Emotive Imagery" in the Treatment of Children's Phobias. *Journal of Mental Science,* 1962, Vol. 108, pp. 191–195.

An Atmosphere for Stories

A story, as with other teaching methods, may not be a one-time thing. If a parent wants to strengthen the child's new behaviors, he may wish to tell the child several stories with the same theme but different content. This will not only increase the likelihood that the story will be effective in changing the child's behavior, but it might also increase the generality of the behavioral change. Telling several stories where the theme remains the same but the specific content varies is similar to using observational learning methods to teach rule-governed behavior which were mentioned in Chapter 10. Remember, one suggestion for teaching rule-governed behavior was to vary the modeled example, but keep the rule the same. An example of this was when the parent of a retarded girl was teaching her daughter appropriate ways of greeting different people. The mother invited several people to visit the home and modeled correct greeting behavior for her daughter.

Telling a child several different stories can accomplish the same purpose. The rule or behavior will be repeated, but the context of the behavior will vary.

What should the child's environment be like when he is told a teaching story? In the above example, when Tom's father told him the story about rescuing a dog, the story was told just before the child went to bed. The child had just had a warm bath and was drinking a glass of juice while sitting on his father's lap listening to his father tell the story. This is a nice setting for a story. The child is comfortable, relaxed, and probably feels very happy to be snuggled into his father's lap. Although it might not be absolutely necessary, a warm, trusting environment is probably a very good setting for telling a story. In this setting the child might not only learn the desired behavior, but he will probably gain from the good feelings of being close to someone he loves. Even if this is all that is accomplished by telling the story, real gains may have been made in the child's relationship with others.

As was mentioned earlier, a good story is one that will keep the child's attention. In fact, a parent should not become so concerned with the moral or the teaching component of the story that its entertainment value is lost. Children learn best in a situation that is interesting to them. One way that I've found to increase the interest in the story, and possibly the teaching value of a story, is to let the child participate in the story. For example, let's return to the story about

Tom and the dog and see how the father might have included Tom in a more active role in telling the story. After Tom and his father arrived at the cave and found out what was the matter, Tom's father might have said to Tom, "What do you think could be done?" The child, because of his fear of dogs, might suggest several alternatives, such as calling the fire department. When the child makes suggestions that avoid engaging in the behavior, the father could deftly discourage these suggestions by saying such things as "The firemen couldn't get their truck into the woods." Then the father might suggest, "To save time don't you think it might be best if Tom went into the cave to get the dog? He is the only one around who is small enough."

An advantage of trying to get the child to commit himself is that when a person is responsible for a decision he is more likely to engage in the relevant behaviors. When someone else makes the decision there is less demand on the person to do the behaviors. Another reason why the child should be encouraged to participate in the story is that he might provide alternative ways of handling the problem that are better than those the father suggests. This is similar to using the SOCS method mentioned in Chapter 3 where the parent helps the child decide what options are available and the consequences of the various options.

If a parent chooses to have the child participate in the story, he should develop the participation over several stories. The first story might require little child participation, the next story more, and so on, until the child is taking a very active role. I've used this approach and found that with a little experience a child can often carry the story by himself. All I had to do was occasionally bring the story back to the problem. It worked beautifully. The child's behavior not only improved, but his ability to look at the problem and develop ways of handling the problem were also very much improved.

SELF-CONTROL

What is a parent trying to do when teaching a child to talk to himself? What is a parent attempting to do when he tells a teaching story? Probably the parent is not only trying to change a specific behavior, but he is also trying to teach his child how to handle new problems. The parent is trying to teach the child self-control.

For many children most of their behavior is directed by others. We tell our children, "Get ready for school," or "It's time to eat," or "Don't do that Johnny, it's dumb." We direct our child's behavior because the child is either incapable of directing his own behavior or because we haven't taught him to control his own behavior. Because children are constantly learning and changing, both control from parent and self-control are probably desirable and necessary. External control is important when a child is encountering new things in the world. He simply doesn't know how to react. Self-control, on the other hand, can be learned and used by the child in many situations. For example, most children after they reach a certain age don't require their parents to tell them to go to the bathroom. They learn how to control their own behavior.

A child learns self-control over a period of time by first observing his parents and responding to their cues. As the child grows older and gains mastery of his language, he is more and more able to replace his parent's instructions with his own. At first, the child directs his own behavior by talking out loud to himself. Later the self-control is guided by the child's thinking or private talk.

A parent who wants to teach his child to control his own behavior should keep this developmental function in mind. If a parent is trying to teach his three-year-old child to "think" about what he was doing, the child might fail to gain control over his behavior. He simply wouldn't be prepared to make the jump from parent instructions to private instructions.

Similarly, if you want to teach an older child to control his own behavior, you should make sure that his aloud self-instructions are adequate. If they are, you can then proceed to teach the child to privately self-instruct. You might encourage private self-instructions by having the child whisper the self-instructions before he instructs silently.

In summary, teaching a child to talk to himself or telling a child a story where he is shown ways of reacting to situations are both ways of teaching a child to control his own behavior. These are not the only methods of teaching a child self-control. Most of the teaching methods we have discussed in the book can be used to teach self-control. For example, a child could be taught to control his anger in several ways: the parent could talk to the child; the parent could punish the child; the parent could reward the child for nonangry behavior; or the parent could model nonangry behavior. The choice of the method used would depend upon which has worked in the past with the child and the speed with which the parent wants to reduce the child's angry behavior.

The parent usually wants to do more than teach a child to engage in a given behavior; he wants the child to be able to handle new situations. One way of increasing the likelihood of a child engaging in the desired behavior in new situations is to train the child to control his own behavior rather than depend on external sources of control. Teaching methods that are intentionally designed to increase a child's control over his own behavior are more likely to help the child handle new situations.

IMAGINATION AND ROLE-PLAYING

A fun teaching method that is similar in many ways to having the child participate in telling a story is for you and your child to role-play various interpersonal interactions. When people role-play they intentionally take on roles that are somewhat contrived for the purpose of showing how they see another person's behavior or to show someone different ways of behaving. For example, a mother and her daughter might role-play being one another. In this situation the mother tries to behave as she sees her daughter behaving; the daughter responds as she sees her mother behaving. This can have the interesting effect of letting you see how your child perceives your role and your actions toward her. You may find that your child sees your behavior differently than you do. You can also use your behavior to illuminate some of your child's inappropriate behaviors. If you properly act out the way your child behaves, she may see how inappropriate her behaviors are and you or the child can suggest ways of changing.

Let's look at an example of a mother and daughter who have exchanged roles for the evening. Before role-playing the mother had suggested that after they role-play they talk about how they perceived each other in their new roles. The mother had intentionally structured this review of each other's roles so that she might point out to her child that she had been behaving in a nasty way in recent weeks. It seemed to the mother that whenever she asked her daughter to help around the house, the daughter would reply by saying, "Oh, mother! I'm too busy."

This role-playing scene begins after dinner:

Daughter: Julia, would you come and help me with the dishes? I need some
              help.
Mother: Oh, Mom! I'm busy. Why do you always ask me? Why don't
              you ask Jeff or Dad?

With these opening statements each is saying what the other person typically says. The next statements will allow each person a chance to react as they would want the other person to behave.

Daughter: OK, you're right. Sometimes I do ask you to do things just
              because you are a girl. I suppose it is right for all of us to share in
              the household chores.
Mother: Well, I will help you. Sometimes I forget that you are the one
              who usually gets stuck with the dishes after dinner.

In this simple little exchange each person stated why they behave as they do. The daughter complains when the mother asks for help because she feels she is being discriminated against because she is a girl. The mother gets upset when the daughter refuses to help because she feels that she is always being stuck with cleaning up after a meal while everyone else is enjoying themselves. Although most role-playing episodes are much longer than this, let's look at the review discussion between the mother and her daughter on just this portion of the role-playing episode:

Mother: Julia, do you really feel that I'm being unfair when I ask you to
              help? I really hadn't thought I was. I know I ask you to help with
              the dishes more than I ask Jeff or your father, but I guess I
              always felt doing dishes was a woman's job.
Daughter: I really wouldn't mind helping you, but it makes me mad to see
              Jeff and Dad in the living room while I'm stuck in here doing
              dishes.
Mother: I know what you mean. I guess that's why I ask you to help. If
              you don't help, then you are in the living room and I'm here by
              myself. I ask you because you're a girl, I guess.

This brief discussion following the role-playing episode brought out why each person was behaving as they were. Originally the mother had simply labeled her daughter's behavior as being "nasty," but was unaware what was causing it. If pushed to explain her daughter's behavior, the mother might have said, "I suppose it is just a stage she is going through." Now, after role-playing and discussing their reactions to one another, the mother was able to see that her daughter's "nasty" behavior was produced by the same factors that made her ask for the daughter's help: they both feel it is unfair for the others to be relaxing while they work. With the factors causing each person's actions better illuminated, each can suggest ways of altering the situation so that their behavior is more appropriate.

Another way in which role-playing can be used to help a child improve his behavior is to have the child role-play himself in various problem behavior situations. Imagine a child who has been having problems getting along with his teacher. The child complains to his parents that the teacher is always picking on him and won't let him talk in class. The child's mother suggested that she play the role of his teacher and her husband play the role of one of the classmates and the boy play himself. While the mother was role-playing the classroom scene she notices that her child would sometimes sneer and shake his head when she asked her husband a question and the answer was not quite correct. When she asked the son to give his answer he would start off by saying the other student was wrong and then give the correct answer.

After observing this example of the child's classroom behavior, the mother understands why his teacher might be annoyed. The boy was obviously being rude to his classmates. Once the mother finds why her child is having trouble with his teacher she might wish to explain what she observed and help him practice or role-play other ways of answering questions. She might have the child practice not sneering and, if the answer given by a classmate was generally correct, nodding his head in agreement. When he was called on he could then say that his classmate was generally correct, but he had some additions. The child, because he was concerned with the way his teacher was reacting, might agree that this is a better approach.

Role-playing has several important features which recommend its usage. It gives the child a chance to practice different ways of behaving in the same setting and getting the "feel" of each different behavior before he actually enters the situation. This practice will make him feel more confident when he is required to do the behavior. Consider how much better a child who has to give a report to his class might feel if he has already practiced with you as an audience.

Another advantage is that you can give your children immediate and precise feedback on their behavior. In the example of the child who was having problems with his teacher, his mother was able to recognize that he was "putting down" his classmates. He might have been unaware of this, but her feedback helped him identify the behavior and make changes.

Finally, role-playing allows the child a chance to practice doing things where he feels incompetent. By role-playing he will not only build his confidence, but will also acquire skills that are necessary for the desired behavior.

EXAMPLE 11.1

Imaginative Use of a Child's Imagination

An imaginative parent can not only help his child acquire appropriate behaviors, but he can make the learning situation very enjoyable. Sometimes, these enjoyable strategies are very effective for teaching children. Drs. Lazarus and Abramovitz were able to capitalize on a "game" idea to create a very interesting treatment program for a ten-year-old boy who was afraid of the dark. The boy's fear developed shortly after seeing a frightening movie and then being cautioned by his grandmother not to go near doors and windows at night because of robbers and kidnappers. The boy's fear of the dark made him an object of ridicule and created difficulties with his parents.

During treatment sessions Lazarus and Abramovitz found that the boy greatly admired two radio serial heroes, Superman and Captain Silver. These characters were incorporated into the child's treatment program. The child was told to close his eyes, imagine that he was an agent of Captain Silver and Superman, and imagine that he received a call from them on his secret radio. To answer the call, the child was told to imagine, for example, that he had to go into a dimly lit hallway. These imaginary scenes were terminated if the child indicated that he was anxious.

After three sessions the child was able to imagine himself alone in his bathroom with the lights off waiting for a call from Captain Silver and Superman.

The treatment program was effective in ridding the child of his fear of the dark. In addition, several other positive changes were noted: the child's schoolwork improved, and he did not seem so insecure. This case study shows that not only can the child's imagination be used to help teach the child new behaviors, but an imaginative parent can create learning situations that are not only enjoyable but effective for teaching the child.

From A. A. Lazarus and A. Abramovitz, The Use of Emotive Imagery in the Treatment of Children's Phobias. *Journal of Mental Science*, 1962, Vol. 108, pp. 191–195.

EXERCISE

Role-playing is a terrific device for finding out why a person behaves in certain ways. Role-playing can also be used to teach new and more appropriate behavior. In this exercise I will provide several guidelines for using role-playing. You may find that you will have to adjust conditions slightly for different problems, but the guidelines will give you an excellent start in using role-playing to improve your interactions with your children.

1. Explaining role-playing. In most situations role-playing should be introduced to your children as an effort *to help them find better ways of behaving in specific situations*. This can be handled as described in the problem-solving section of Chapter 3. It is important that this helpful procedure not be perceived as punishment by your child.

2. Setting the scene. Usually it is a good idea to let the child "direct" the scene. After all, one thing you are trying to find out is why the child behaves inappropriately. This requires that you try to *see the situation through his eyes*. One way of helping the child "set the scene" is to have the child close his eyes and imagine what happened. Then have him describe it. Let me give an example of how this can be done:

Mother: OK, son, close your eyes and try to remember what happened when you and Mike had your argument. What was happening? When you think you remember, tell me about it. Then we'll try to act out what was happening.

If you do this, listen carefully to what the child said and try to role-play the scene exactly as he described it. *Don't add what you think happened.*

3. Role-playing. If the purpose of your role-playing is to not only find out what happened, but also to teach more appropriate behaviors, then you should do the following: (a) After the scene has been role-played, point out to the child which behaviors were appropriate. *Find something positive to comment on.* Then point out a more appropriate way of handling those behaviors that were less appropriate. Just select one or two items. (b) Go through the scene again, but *this time have the child role-play the more appropriate ways of behaving.* Again compliment the child on his good points—especially any improvements before bringing up less appropriate behaviors. (c) Continue working on behaviors that were not appropriate.

These guidelines for role-playing are simple, but point out its main features for teaching new behaviors. It can be a very effective method of getting to know your children and teaching the new behaviors.

12

Professional Help For Disturbed Children

THE CHILD WITH PROBLEMS

Sometimes, because of either events in the family beyond a parent's control (such as a child being separated from his family), or problems between a child's parents, or a child's illness, the child can develop behavior problems that might require help beyond that which his parents are able to offer. These problem behaviors can often occur in spite of how hard we try to teach children appropriate behaviors. Various professionals have estimated that approximately 10 percent of the school-age children in the United States could benefit from some form of professional psychological help. Hopefully, some day this figure will be smaller as we find out more about why children develop severe behavioral problems and as parents become more effective in teaching their children how to interact with their world. But regardless of the effect of improved parenting skills, there will still be a sizable

176

number of children who could benefit from professional help. What are parents to do if they feel their child could profit from professional help?

Attitudes Toward Behavior Problems

Parents will often delay taking their child to a psychologist or other professionals in the treatment of children with behavioral or emotional problems because they feel their child's problems reflect on their capabilities as a parent. If I have done an adequate job in this book, I should have communicated the idea that a person is not born a good parent: good parenting practices must be learned. Some people have an advantage over others because, as children, their parents were capable of teaching them positive ways of interacting with others that later became good parenting practices. Other people were not so lucky and were brought up in home environments that were less likely to produce the behaviors that would be effective when they became parents.

Many people, in spite of not having the most desirable models as parents, have nevertheless become good parents. They may have had experiences with their children, friends, or relatives that helped them develop good parenting skills, or they may have learned the necessary skills in school or other places.

If, however, a person did not have an opportunity to develop these skills by having positive experiences, this does not mean they intentionally became parents who encouraged their children to engage in inappropriate behaviors. On the contrary, many times when we make mistakes with our children it is because we either did not have adequate knowledge or we did what we thought was best without realizing the effect we were having on children. And most important, some of the behavior problems children have are not due to inappropriate parenting practices, but are due to things such as illness and other factors the parent is unable to control.

PROFESSIONAL HELP

Regardless of why a child has problems, we should not have the attitude that his parents are bad parents. We have seen in this book that many of our children's behaviors can be changed when we use good teaching methods. The same is true for parents. If a parent has unwittingly had an effect on his child's behavior that is undesirable, a professional can often help the parent learn new ways of interacting with his child that will not only reduce his child's problems but also improve the parent's skills. To allow ourselves not to seek the help of a professional when we feel it is necessary (just because we are concerned with what our friends might say) is to do a disservice to ourselves and our children. Seeking the help of a professional when it is necessary, rather than being an indication of being a poor parent, is an indication of positive parental concern. A parent's attempts to help his child who has behavior or emotional problems is every bit as positive as taking him to a medical doctor when he has a medical problem.

How to Find Professional Help

If your child does have behavioral or emotional problems, where can you go to get good professional help? There are several places you might consider. If your child is of school age, you could ask the school principal to refer you to the school counselor. If the school doesn't have a qualified professional counselor, the school district probably does. If the school recommends a counselor, you might wish to visit with him and explain your concerns. The counselor may feel that it is out of his jurisdiction or range of competency, but he might refer you to someone who is more qualified to handle the problem.

A second source of recommedations would be your family doctor or religious leader. It is likely that they have made other, similar referrals and can recommend a competent professional to you. Most medical doctors and religious leaders won't try to do professional psychological counseling. They simply haven't been trained for it, but they are often aware of professionals who are capable of handling your problems.

A third source of help would be a local university. Most universities employ psychologists and other professionals who might be able to provide you with the help you or your child needs. Some university teachers of psychology are too busy to do counseling or therapy, but they usually can refer you to someone who is highly qualified.

Fourth, many community, county, state, and federal agencies are available to provide help. Some of these agencies don't offer the services you need, but can recommend appropriate agencies. Some of the government agencies you might wish to contact are mental health centers, welfare agencies, child development services, and family services. These can be found listed in your telephone book.

Finally, you might have friends who have taken their child to a professional for help. If so, ask them. They will probably be able to recommend someone who is competent.

When you decide upon a professional you might wish to visit him before taking your child to him. This initial visit will allow you to explain the problem to the professional, and he will be able to tell you if he is able to handle the problem and how he might go about doing it. This information will allow you to decide if you would feel comfortable having this person working with you and your child. This initial visit will also give you an opportunity to check the professional's credentials. Unfortunately, in some states the laws governing who can practice psychotherapy are inadequate. This has the feature of allowing some people who are inadequately trained to act as counselors or psychotherapists. Another problem is that many people who are not certified to provide psychological services are still doing it under a different name. You have the right to question the person's credentials. Is he licensed to practice psychotherapy? Has he had training in treating the types of problems you are presenting to him? Qualified people will not hesitate to assure you of their qualifications. Ask—it's your right.

What to Expect from a Professional

If you do find a professional that you wish to have help you with your child's behavior problems, what can you expect from him? In other words, what will he ask of you and of your child? What approach will he use to try to help correct the problem? Answers to these questions are very difficult because psychologists and others who work with children and families have different approaches. But I will try to summarize briefly some of the major types of things that different therapists might do. Remember, the particular therapist that you select might do none of the things I describe, or he may combine several of the different approaches. I personally feel that you should find out what approach the therapist uses, and if you find it acceptable you might be able to work with him more effectively. If on the other hand you have serious reservations about his particular approach, you should tell him. He will either help you to understand what he will be doing and why he thinks it will help, or he may refer you to someone whom he feels you might be more comfortable working with. It is important that you have positive feelings toward the person with whom you will be working. Otherwise, therapy may not proceed as smoothly as it should.

Group or Individual Therapy?

Some therapists will expect you or your child, or possibly both of you, to participate in a therapy group with people who have similar problems. Other professional therapists will prefer to see your child or you or both of you in individual therapy. Which procedure the therapist selects will depend on how effective he feels each would be for your particular problem and the therapist's feelings of which method he can use most effectively.

If you or your child are asked to participate in a group, what can you expect? Again, there are different types of groups, and what is done in the group setting will depend upon the professional who is directing the group. One very common group procedure is where the group is composed of the family unit. The therapist in this situation may want to meet not only with the child and his parents, but also with the other children in the family. Basically, the idea behind this approach is that conditions in the family which have had an effect on one child might also be having an effect on other members of the family. By bringing the family together as a group the therapist can often help members of the family see where there are interactional failures and show how the behavior of each member of the family is affecting the behavior of others in the family. With this information, the therapist can then help each member of the family to learn more appropriate ways of interacting with the others.

Another common group procedure is where the parents of the child with behavior problems are asked to participate in a group with other parents while the child is seen either in individual therapy or group therapy with other children. The idea behind this is that you might be able to explore, with the help of others who have similar problems, your feelings and ways of acting toward your child. This mutual exploration can often have the effect of helping you understand more completely your relationship with your child and other members of the family. It is also sometimes comforting to find that other parents have problems with their children. This can help reduce feelings of guilt you might have. Once you have discovered something about yourself in relation to your family, the group might be able to help you learn other ways of interacting with your family, or they may affirm the methods you are using.

If your child is asked to participate in a group, he may have experiences similar to those described above (but with children his age), or he may participate in quite a different group. This will depend upon the age of the child, the seriousness of his problems, and other factors. Generally, the older the child and the less severe his problems, the more likely his group will be like that described above. Younger children are generally placed into groups with a different structure. For example, a young child might be placed into a play-therapy group. In this setting the child may be encouraged to play with various toys, and while he is interacting with these objects and the other children the therapist will observe in an attempt to understand why the child is behaving as he is and to teach him more appropriate ways of interacting with his environment.

In individual therapy the person with whom you or your child would interact is the therapist. As with group therapy, the types of interactions between you, or your child, and the therapist will depend on the therapist's frame of reference and the nature of the problem he is trying to help you with.

For convenience, we can classify the types of interactions you or your child might have with a therapist as being either prescriptive or nondirective. These approaches are also used in group situations, but for simplicity they will be only described for individual therapy.

Prescriptive vs. Nondirective Therapy

A therapist who uses a prescriptive approach is likely to give you advice on how to change your behavior and he will probably require you to engage in certain activities. For example, he may prescribe that you record the number of times your child engages in inappropriate behaviors which concern you. After you have completed this task he may recommend that you interact with your child in certain ways whenever the child engages in the inappropriate behavior and a different way when the child is engaging in appropriate behaviors. You might also be asked to record your behavior. He might, for example, have you record how often you praise your child.

The types of prescriptions you receive will depend, of course, on the type of problem you and your child have and the technique he thinks will be most helpful. The point is that the prescriptive therapist will take an active role in having you carry out a variety· of assignments outside the therapy sessions. Sometimes the prescriptions might even take place in the therapy environment. For example, you might be asked to interact with your child and to react to your child's behaviors in specified ways while the therapist is watching.

A nondirective therapist will give you fewer prescriptions or advice. His role will be mainly one of an educated "listener." He will encourage you to talk about yourself, your child, and your relationship with your child and others. By doing this he will be able to help you discover some things about yourself and your feelings toward your children. Once he helps you to explore your self and your relationship with others, he will encourage you to devise better ways of dealing with yourself and your children if this is necessary.

If the therapist chooses to work with your child instead of you or in addition to you, the child will have similar types of interactions with the therapist. But rather than the therapist giving you prescriptions or having you talk about your problems, the child will receive this attention.

Concerns You Might Have

If you have decided that your child could benefit from professional help and you have found a professional whom you are satisfied will be able to help you, you might wish to ask him some additional questions. If you do have questions, it is your right and responsibility to have them answered. If you do not ask such questions, you may have certain expectancies that will not be met and the experience may not be as positive as it should have been. In addition, the answers to the questions can help reduce any anxiety you might have toward entering your child or yourself into the therapeutic situation. I know many people are hesitant to ask questions of people they go to for help. For example, many people are hesitant to ask their medical doctor about what he is doing and why. When we don't ask these questions we sometimes worry unnecessarily. If we had asked the questions, most of our concerns would have been eliminated.

Some of the questions you may wish to ask the person whom you have taken your child to for psychological help are:

1. *How long does the professional expect therapy will take?* This can be a very difficult question for the professional to answer because his experience might have taught him that the child's problem is difficult to work with, or he may be more optimistic and tell you that treatment won't require much time. Regardless of the therapist's answer, you should ask him to set an evaluation date where you, the child, and the professional will sit down and decide how successful therapy has been. At this meeting you and the therapist might decide that therapy is progressing well and should be continued or that the child's problems have been adequately dealt with and therapy should be terminated. Or you might even decide that the therapy has had little effect on the problem and that the therapist should refer the child and you to someone else who might be more effective in handling the problem.

It is only fair when evaluating the progress in therapy to give the therapist, the child, and yourself adequate time to see if the particular therapy is going to be successful. But you should not feel obligated to remain with a particular therapist if he is having no success in correcting the problem. Not all therapists and therapeutic procedures are equally good at treating different problems. A therapist who might be successful in treating some problems might not be as successful with other problems.

2. *What will my child be like, and what will our relationship be like, when we have completed therapy?* In other words, what can you expect from therapy? This again is a difficult question for the therapist to answer, but he should give you some idea of what to expect. As in the case of how long will therapy take, the answer to this question will allow you to evaluate the help you and your child are receiving. If the therapist tells you to expect a certain outcome, then you can decide if he has achieved what you were led to expect. If the expected results haven't been achieved, then you will want to ask why. The answer to this question will allow you to make decisions about how you want to proceed.

When you ask questions (1) and (2), make sure that you understand the answers. If you don't, ask them again.

3. *How much will therapy cost?* As with all professionals, the cost of a psychologist's time can be quite expensive. However, he might be

able to suggest ways in which either part or all of his fee can be deferred. Some health insurance policies make provisions to pay for psychological services. Check yours, it may have such a provision. Other possibilities are that the fees will be paid by welfare or by mental health or family service agencies; you might ask the therapist about these.

If you find that the costs of therapy will be more than you feel you can pay, then you should seriously consider applying to city, county, state, and federal agencies for help. It would be a shame for a person not to receive the help he needs just because he cannot afford it. Your therapist should be able to help you find some agency to help you with payments if this is necessary.

Final Word

As you are already aware, being a good parent can be hard work. I can see where it might be easier for a parent just to give up and let his child develop without direction, but most of us can't do that. We feel we have a responsibility to help our child develop in ways that will make him happy and socially responsible. To do this in our modern society requires that we continually change and grow with our children. The ideas that might have been helpful twenty years ago might not be appropriate in this day and age. We have to work at improving our capabilities as parents.

Those of you who have read this book and other similar books are working. You are trying to find new and better ways of interacting with your child. I admire this effort. Parents who are not concerned with their child's development would be unlikely to spend the time reading a book on child-rearing patterns. This makes you special.

I hope that I have given you some new ideas that might help you interact more positively with your child. I also hope that the ideas in this book have made you a better parent. If they have, then my book has been a success.

Glossary

I feel a glossary should do more than simply define words. Therefore, I will define words as they are used in the text, and where appropriate, I will define the words as professionals use them. In addition, for some words I'll try to give you an example of the context in which the word is used. I hope this will help you to understand each word more fully.

ANXIETY A feeling of being upset or fearful. Unlike fear, however, it is difficult to state what is causing you to be upset. The cues are often vague. Anxiety is a composite response: We show bodily changes such as a hollow feeling in the gut; affective changes of feeling such as worry; and cognitive or thinking changes such as being preoccupied with some thought.

APPROPRIATE BEHAVIOR Appropriate behavior is relative. Appropriate behavior is behavior that is defined as being desirable by a given group of people (including the person engaging in the behavior) in a particular situation. Typically, for young children it is the responsibility of the parents to define what is appropriate. This guidance by the parent will allow the child to determine later if a behavior is appropriate.

AVERSIVE STIMULI   An aversive stimulus is something that happens to us that we subjectively evaluate as unpleasant. What is aversive for one person may not be aversive for another. For example, loud music may be unpleasant for one person but not for another. Aversive stimuli usually produces changes in behavior that cause the aversive stimuli not to occur again. This may be a reduction in behavior (such as behavior that causes a child to be punished) or an increase in behavior that prevents the aversive stimuli from occurring (such as a child picking up his toys so that his parents won't yell at him.)

AVOIDANCE BEHAVIOR   Avoidance behavior is behavior that prevents the occurrence of an aversive stimulus. For example, the child's behavior of picking up his clothes in the above definition is an example of avoidance behavior. The child avoids being yelled at by engaging in an appropriate behavior.

BEHAVIOR   Behavior is whatever we do. Most often we think of behavior as actions that others can observe, such as walking, touching things, and so forth. But other things such as thinking, talking, and changes in bodily states, such as blushing, are also behaviors. For our purposes, however, we are most concerned with behavior that someone including ourselves can observe and change.

BY-PRODUCTS (OF INTERACTIONS)   By-products are changes in behavior, feeling, or thought that occur as an accidental result of an interaction between people. For example, a child who is punished by being spanked for some direct behavior may avoid his parents or say to himself, "I don't like Dad." The avoidance and private conversation are negative by-products. They were not intended to occur when punishment was delivered. Positive by-products also occur. When a child is happy after receiving a reward, he is showing a positive by-product if all that was intended when the behavior was rewarded was to increase how often the behavior occurs.

CONDITIONING   Conditioning means about the same thing as learning. Professionals use conditioning in a slightly more specialized sense to refer to specific sets of laboratory procedures to produce learning. Conditioning can refer to the precise things done to produce a behavior change (process) or the changes in behavior produced by the teaching process (product).

CONSEQUENCE   A behavioral consequence is something that happens to a person as the *result of his behavior*. Consequences can be negative (aversive) or positive (pleasant). These consequences influence whether the behavior is likely to be repeated. For example, if you touch a hot stove, you receive a negative consequence and are unlikely to repeat the behavior. On the other hand, if you comb your hair in a new way and people compliment you (positive consequence), you are likely to continue combing your hair in that style.

CONTROL (OF BEHAVIOR)   Control refers to the fact that behavior is more or less likely to occur in certain situations. For example, a child is more likely to smile and act happy in the presence of people who reward his behavior than in the presence of people who have frequently punished him. In other words, certain situations *influence* how we act. In some situations our behavior is very *predictable* (the situation exerts a high degree of control) and less predictable in others (low degree of control).

COUNTER AGGRESSION   Punishment, whether physical, verbal, or producing isolation, can be perceived by the person being punished as aggressive. If the punishment produces pain or is perceived as unfair, the person being punished will often strike out at the person doing the punishing. This striking out is referred to as counter aggression. It is aggression in response to aggression. There is some evidence that counter aggression is a reflexive response to pain.

COUNTER CONTROL   If a person perceives that his behavior is being influenced or controlled unfairly or in unwarranted ways, the person will try to change the situation. This response to unwarranted control is termed counter control. For example, a child who rebels when he feels unfairly treated may be trying to exert counter control over the situation.

COVERT MODELING   Covert modeling is a teaching procedure in which the child is asked to *imagine someone* (often the child him-or herself) who is similar to him, *engaging in a behavior.* Depending on what is being taught, the child *also imagines appropriate consequences* for the behavior. For example, a child who is afraid of dogs imagines himself approaching a dog and being praised for his approach. Similarly, covert modeling can be used to punish an inappropriate behavior. For example, a child may imagine herself being rude to friends and the friends saying they won't play with her.

DISCRIMINATE (DISCRIMINATION LEARNING)   A child is making a discrimination when he engages in an appropriate behavior in the presence of some cues but not others. For example, a child may have learned a discriminative response of running and yelling when he is on the play ground but not when he is in buildings. A discrimination is taught by reinforcing the behavior in the presence of appropriate cues and not reinforcing the behavior (or punishing the behavior) in the presence of cues indicating that the behavior should not occur.

EMOTIONAL BEHAVIOR   Emotional behavior is composed of three things: bodily reactions, feeling states, and behavior. Emotional behavior can be positive such as "joy." When a child feels joy, his heart rate may increase, he will feel happy, and he will smile, jump, or engage in other relevant behaviors. Emotional behavior can also be negative, such as "anxiety" (see the definition for anxiety). Positive emotional behaviors are often associated with rewards and negative emotional behavior with punishment.

EMPATHY (EMPATHIZE)   Empathy occurs when we can "experience" what another person is feeling, thinking, or doing in a particular situation. We can empathize with others because we have had similar feelings and thoughts or have engaged in similar behaviors when we were in similar situations. A child's ability to empathize with others is important when modeling or covert modeling teaching procedures are being used. Empathy is also important for the parent who is trying to understand why a child is engaging in particular behavior.

EXTINCTION   Extinction refers to two things. First it refers to a method of decreasing how often a behavior occurs. To extinguish a behavior we remove the rewards that the behavior has been producing. For example, if a child has been getting attention for throwing a tantrum, the attention now no longer is forthcoming when the tantrum occurs. Extinction also refers to the reduction in behavior. If the behavior no longer occurs after rewards have been removed, we say the behavior has extinguished.

GENERALIZATION   When a person engages in a behavior in the presence of similar cues, we can say he is generalizing. For example, a child who smiles when he meets friends, relatives, friends of parents, and neighbors is showing generalized smiling. Generalization is the opposite of discrimination. For some behaviors we wish the behavior to occur only in the presence of one (or a few) cues (discrimination); other behaviors we wish to have occur in the presence of many cues (generalization). Generalization is taught by rewarding the child for engaging in the desired behavior in the presence of many, similar cues.

GOAL BEHAVIOR   Goal behavior refers to the behavior we wish to teach. When we begin to teach a child to use a more appropriate behavior, we often must first teach intermediate behaviors. These intermediate behaviors are only approximations to the goal behavior. For any teaching program we should be able to state precisely what the goal behavior is that we are trying to teach.

IMAGINATION   Imagination refers to how a child can, in his "mind's eye," visualize himself or others engaging in various behaviors and the consequences of the behaviors. In a teaching context this allows the child to visualize himself engaging in a variety of behaviors. By imagining the behavior he can, in a sense, practice the behaviors without actually performing them.

IMITATION   Imitation is the copying of a model's behavior. When a child imitates a model, he may imitate exactly, partially, or the general pattern of behavior. Imitation occurs when the child has previously been rewarded for imitative behavior or by observing a model being rewarded for the behavior. Imitative learning probably accounts for most of a child's learned behavior.

INAPPROPRIATE BEHAVIOR   As with appropriate behavior, inappropriate behavior is relative to the situation. A behavior that is inappropriate in one situation may not be in another. Generally, however, a behavior can be considered inappropriate for the situation if it will cause harm to the child, make the child (or others) unhappy, or cause damage to someone or something. For most behaviors it is easy to decide if they are inappropriate. For example, most would agree that hitting (with intent to hurt), stealing, and lying are inappropriate. Other behaviors are more difficult to determine. For example, loud talk and expressions of anger are sometimes appropriate, sometimes not. A parent must trust his or her judgment for such behavior. The reaction to such behavior should be consistent, however.

INCOMPATIBLE BEHAVIOR   When the child is engaged in incompatible behavior, he cannot be doing another behavior. Parents often try to increase behaviors incompatible with less desirable behaviors. For example, a parent may wish to increase cooperative play that is incompatible with aggressive, isolate play. By strengthening a positive behavior that is incompatible with an inappropriate behavior, a parent can use a positive approach rather than a negative approach such as punishment to teach the child.

INFERIORITY COMPLEX   An inferiority complex is a group of feelings and behaviors in which the child engages that are self-punishing and do not match the reality of the situation. For example, a child who does not play with other children and may say, "I am not as good as they are," may be considered to have an inferiority complex. Often a child engages in these behaviors when he has either been punished frequently for not matching the behavior of others (or his parents' expectations) or has frequently been rewarded (attention) for engaging in these "inferiority" behaviors.

INSIGHT   Insight refers to being able to discriminate the factors influencing some action. Typically the action is your own behavior. Often we refer to insight as occurring suddenly and unexpectedly. For example, a person who has had insight into why he behaves in a certain way may say, "I just realized why I've been acting angry with John."

ISOLATION   Isolation is a punishment procedure. When using isolation, a parent may make his child sit in a corner for five minutes. The sitting in the corner removes or isolates the child from potentially rewarding activities. When isolation follows an occurrence of a behavior, the behavior usually occurs less often in the future. Research has shown that brief periods of isolation, say five to ten minutes, is usually as effective as longer isolation periods.

LEARNING   Learning refers to relatively permanent behavior produced by changes either in antecedent cues or behavioral consequences. Using a new word or way of greeting people would constitute learned behavior. Crying when hurt generally would not be learned behavior.

MODEL   A model is a person whose behavior is copied or imitated by another person. Typically the model is a person admired by the person doing the imitating.

MODELING   Modeling refers to demonstrating a behavior that is copied or imitated by another person. Modeling need not be intentional. Any action by a model may be imitated if the model is rewarded for the behavior or if the person imitating is rewarded for copying the behavior. There is good evidence that most behaviors learned by a child are learned through the process of modeling.

MOTIVATION   Motivation usually refers to two different things. First, it means those things that energize or increase the frequency of a person's engaging in a behavior. For example, a child may say, "I want to do well in school because my mother will be proud of me." Here the child's desire to make his mother proud is "motivating" or increases behaviors to do well in school. Second, motivation refers to factors that direct behavior. For example, a person may say, "Boy, I'm hungry. I'm going to go in the kitchen and fix myself a sandwich." Being hungry not only energized behavior; it also directed (go to the kitchen) the behavior. A careful analysis will show that most of the factors motivating our behavior can be shown to be antecedent stimuli and behavioral consequences.

OBSERVATIONAL LEARNING   Observational learning means the same thing as modeling. Both refer to a process that occurs when one person learns to engage in a behavior (or not engage in the behavior) by observing someone else engage in that behavior.

OVERCORRECTION   Overcorrection is a punishment procedure in which the person being punished is required to correct his action and improve the situation to a "better than before" condition. For example, a child who wrote on a wall with a crayon may be made to wash off the crayon marks *and* clean an additional part of the wall. Overcorrection is effective because the child cannot be enjoying more rewarding activities while he is correcting his behavior. In addition, the child is also required to practice a more appropriate behavior.

PARENTING   Parenting refers to relatively long-term interactions between an adult and child that influence the child's future behavior. Parenting behavior can be intentional or unintentional; it can be positive or negative, and it can be behavior that directly or indirectly influences a child's behavior. Examples of parenting behaviors are included in the text of this book.

POSITIVE PRACTICE   Positive practice is a teaching technique in which a child is required to practice repeatedly an appropriate response. Positive practice usually occurs following an instance of inappropriate behavior. When the inappropriate behavior occurs, rather than the child being punished (or following punishment), he is required to positively practice a more appropriate behavior. For example, if a child had a bowel accident in his pants, he may be required to positively practice going to the bathroom, taking down his pants, sitting on the toilet, straining, wiping, flushing the toilet, and so on. Normally there would be at least five positive practice episodes.

PSYCHOTHERAPIST   The term psychotherapist, as used in the book, refers to any person who is trained in behavior change procedures. Normally, a psychotherapist would be a psychiatrist (a medical doctor trained in behavior change procedures), a psychologist (usually with a Ph.D, or sometimes a M.A. and training in behavior change), or a psychiatric social worker trained in behavior change procedures. A psychotherapist's job is to help determine if behavior problems exist, who has the problem, and to help correct the problem. Different psychotherapists will approach these tasks in different ways.

PSYCHOTHERAPY   Psychotherapy can be broadly thought of as a group of techniques that can be used to remediate or correct behavior problems or teach a person appropriate behaviors. Different psychotherapists will use different techniques, and the same therapist will use different techniques for different problems. The various chapters in the book provide examples of some of the things a psychotherapist may do during psychotherapy.

PROMPTINGS   Promptings are special cues that are provided to a person when he is learning a new behavior. As the behavior becomes more efficient, the promptings are withdrawn. For example, a child who is trying to learn a

new word—say, "psychotherapist"—may receive the prompt, "psychoth
. . ." from his teacher. If the child correctly finishes the word, he may be
asked to repeat the full word or part of the word following a smaller prompt-
ing, say, "psy . . . ."

PUNISHMENT   Punishment is the delivery of an aversive event, following
an instance of behavior, which reduces the frequency of future occurrences of
that behavior. The most important aspects of punishment are: (1) It follows
the behavior, and (2) it reduces the frequency of future occurrences of the
behavior. Many things can be used as punishers. For example, a parent can
punish a child by spanking her, sending her to her room, or yelling at her. If
these parental activities reduce the future occurrences of the punished
behavior, they fit the definition of punishment.

REFLEXIVE BEHAVIOR   Reflexive behavior can be thought of as
behavior that we engage in without conscious intention. These behaviors are
usually defensive and intended to remove us from harm. If, for example, we
touch a hot stove, we immediately withdraw our hand. This is a reflex.
Similarly, sometimes we react with rage or aggressive responses to pain.
These responses are not usually consciously willed but occur automatically to
the stimuli.

REINFORCEMENT   Reinforcment is a technical term with a meaning
similar to reward. A reinforcer is an event or thing which, when it follows an
instance of behavior, increases the likelihood of future occurrences of that
behavior. Reinforcement usually refers to the act of delivering the reinforcing
event or object.

REWARD   See reinforcement. A reward can be used to increase the frequency with which a behavior occurs. For example, if praising a person for
his work increases how often he engages in work behavior, then praise is a
reward.

REWARD MENU   A reward menu is a list, a series of pictures, or a combination of the two that describes potential rewards available for engaging in
specific behaviors. Often the different items on the menu require different
amounts of task output for their purchase. A child may, for example, be told
he can watch one hour of television if he completes 20 arithmetic problems,
play catch with his father for a half hour if he completes 15 problems, and so
on. These activities constitute the reward menu. The advantage of the menu is
its variety. The child should always be able to find one of the activities rewarding.

ROLE-PLAYING   Role-playing is a teaching procedure in which a person
learning a new behavior, especially social behaviors, practices the role with
his teacher or parents before trying it in the real world. For example, a shy
child may pretend he is asking another child to spend the night at his house.
The child's parent may take the role of the child to be invited. Role-playing
allows the parent to show the child behavior appropriate to the situation. The
child also has an opportunity to practice the behavior before actually engaging in it in the real situation.

SELF-FULFILLING PROPHECY   When a person is frequently told he behaves in some way, the person often adopts behaviors consistent with the prophecy. For example, a child who is frequently told "you are a nice boy, you play so nicely with your friends," may, in fact, begin to be "nice" and "play nicely with his friends." The opposite prophecy may also influence a child's behavior. A child who is frequently told he is a "bad boy" may begin acting badly.

SELF-INSTRUCTION   Self-instructions occur when we direct our own behavior by talking to ourselves. Sometimes we do this by talking aloud, other times by thinking to ourselves. For example, a child may say to himself, "I'd better not play with dad's tools without asking him. He might get mad." By saying this to himself, the child probably stopped himself from engaging in a behavior that might be punished. The child, therefore, engaged in a purposeful act of self-control. Sometimes children can exert more control over their behavior if they are taught self-instruction techniques.

SHAPING   Shaping technically refers to rewarding successive approximations to a desired behavior. For example, if we wish to teach a child to tie her shoes, we would first reward simply crossing the laces. Later we would require the child to cross the laces and form a bow before rewarding her. We would continue to reward in a similar manner until the child was performing the complete behavior. Shaping is a procedure that allows us to teach complex behaviors in the simplest manner possible.

STIMULUS   Stimulus is a technical term that is basically equivalent to the term *cue*. A stimulus is an antecedent event or thing that influences us to behave in particular ways. For example, a parent's frown is often a stimulus for a child to stop a behavior he is engaging in. Similarly, a red traffic light is a stimulus for a person driving a car to stop the car. A stimulus gains its power to influence behavior when a behavior receives predictable consequences in the presence of the stimulus. For example, a child may have learned to stop some behavior when his parent is frowning because, in the past, a frown was associated with punishment if the behavior persisted.

STIMULUS INFLUENCE   See Control (of behavior)

SYSTEMATIC DESENSITIZATION   Systematic desensitization is a teaching procedure that has been shown to be especially effective for reducing fears. In systematic desensitization, a person is taught to engage in some behavior that is incompatible with fear or anxiety (e.g., deep relaxation) and then is presented the object he fears. The fear object is first presented in a weak form, then in a stronger and stronger form if the person does not show anxiety or fear.

UNCONDITIONAL POSITIVE REGARD   Unconditional positive regard is the ability to like or respect a person for what he is regardless of the behavior he may engage in. A parent, for example, who can communicate through actions and words that she loves and respects her child even though the child may occasionally engage in inappropriate behavior is showing unconditional positive regard. This does not mean the parent should not discipline the child for inappropriate behavior or that the parent must be happy with inappropriate behavior. Rather, it means the parent should love the *child* but not necessarily some of the child's *behavior*.

VERBAL BEHAVIOR   Verbal behavior can refer to any action by a person that communicates information to another person. For example, verbal behavior can include speech, writing, gestures, and so on. Usually, however, we think of verbal behavior as speech.

VERBAL PUNISHMENT   Verbal punishment occurs when a parent yells at his child, criticizes his child, or in some other way reduces the frequency of a child's behavior that is followed by the parent's verbal behavior.

VICARIOUS REWARDS   Vicarious rewards are those we find desirable, that are delivered to another person. Observing a person engage in a behavior that produces vicarious rewards will increase the likelihood that we will engage in a similar behavior.

INDEX